T0312273

Cambridge Elements ⊒

Elements in New Religious Movements
Series Editor
Rebecca Moore
San Diego State University
Founding Editor
†James R. Lewis
Wuhan University

SHAMANIC MATERIALITIES IN NORDIC CLIMATES

Trude Fonneland
*The Arctic University Museum of Norway,
UiT – the Arctic University of Norway*

Tiina Äikäs
University of Oulu

CAMBRIDGE
UNIVERSITY PRESS

CAMBRIDGE
UNIVERSITY PRESS

Shaftesbury Road, Cambridge CB2 8EA, United Kingdom

One Liberty Plaza, 20th Floor, New York, NY 10006, USA

477 Williamstown Road, Port Melbourne, VIC 3207, Australia

314–321, 3rd Floor, Plot 3, Splendor Forum, Jasola District Centre,
New Delhi – 110025, India

103 Penang Road, #05–06/07, Visioncrest Commercial, Singapore 238467

Cambridge University Press is part of Cambridge University Press & Assessment,
a department of the University of Cambridge.

We share the University's mission to contribute to society through the pursuit of
education, learning and research at the highest international levels of excellence.

www.cambridge.org
Information on this title: www.cambridge.org/9781009376402

DOI: 10.1017/9781009376396

First published 2023

A catalogue record for this publication is available from the British Library.

ISBN 978-1-009-37640-2 Paperback
ISSN 2635-232X (online)
ISSN 2635-2311 (print)

Shamanic Materialities in Nordic Climates

Elements in New Religious Movements

DOI: 10.1017/9781009376396
First published online: August 2023

Trude Fonneland
The Arctic University Museum of Norway,
UiT – the Arctic University of Norway

Tiina Äikäs
University of Oulu

Author for correspondence: Trude Fonneland, Trude.fonneland@uit.no

Abstract: This Element takes its starting point in shamanism in the Nordic countries and explores expressions and the lives of shamanic materialities in contemporary Finland and Norway. Shamans interact with spiritual powers and beings, but their religious practices unfold in a material reality. This Element begins with the materiality of shamanism and focuses on how the drum, the sacrificial site, the power animal, and a mushroom bridge the gap between the profane and the divine and create networks and dynamics in a shamanic worldview as well as in the wider society. Throughout its sections, this Element inquires into the ways the construction of the category shamanism makes shamanic materialities come to life. And, in contrast, it examines how shamanic materialities form shamanism and facilitate constantly formative exchanges and dynamics between the local and global, past and present, secular and spiritual, time and space.

Keywords: shamanism, drums, power animals, sacred places, Saami

ISBNs: 9781009376402 (PB), 9781009376396 (OC)
ISSNs: 2635-232X (online), 2635-2311 (print)

Contents

Introduction

Our starting point is shamanism in the north and, more precisely, the expressions of shamanic materialities in contemporary Finland and Norway. Shamans interact with spiritual powers and beings, but their religious practices unfold in a material reality. Compared to textual studies – the study of dogmas and theology – the materiality of religions has been less examined.[1] In this Element, we begin with the materiality of shamanism and focus on how the drum, the sacrificial site, the power animal, and the mushroom bridge the gap between the profane and the divine and create networks and dynamics in a shamanic worldview as well as in the wider society. The shamanic objects in focus in this project are part of different networks that consist of human as well as nonhuman agents, or actants in Latour's terminology. Our aim is to explore the agency of things and their relationships, movements, and transformations, as well as the values, feelings, and obsessions that inform shamans' understanding and use of selected materialities (see Morgan 2009). In this context, shamanic materialities are viewed as active parts in various networks stretching over time and space. The materialities also point to the mobility of religion and the formations and circulation of religion in wider contexts, such as popular culture, tourism, and politics.

We study the circulations of shamanic materialities inspired by Thomas Tweed's definition of religion as "confluences of organic-cultural flows that intensify joy and confront suffering by drawing on human and suprahuman forces to make homes and cross boundaries" (Tweed 2006: 54). An equally important inspiration is David Chidester's *Religion: Material Dynamics* (2018), which offers a timely focus on how circulations of "religious" materialities "require new ways of thinking about religious change and diffusion, religious mobility and plasticity, beyond the frameworks provided by religious institutions" (Chidester 2018: 9).

Shamanic materialities can be simultaneously commodities, spiritual rituals, and transformative political projects. These contexts are not necessarily mutually exclusive, nor are they without occasional contradictions and tensions. The drum, sacrificial sites, power animals, and the mushroom are in this context messengers that enable a dialogue between the past and the present. As folklorist Jonas Frykman says about the role of objects in cultural production: "Things like this – and many more – have become something more than symbols. They

---

[1] In recent decades, the material aspect of religion has nevertheless gained more attention, which can be seen in books like *Religion and Material Culture: The Matter of Belief* (Morgan 2009); *Material Religion and Popular Culture* (King 2010); and *Stuff* (Miller 2010); in 2005, the journal *Material Religion: The Journal of Objects, Art and Belief* was founded.

bear secrets and have to be induced to speak" (Frykman 2002: 49). An overall question explored in this Element is thus how different forms of materialities shape shamanism and, in contrast, how the materialities discussed in the following sections are formed by shamanism.

Our backgrounds in religious studies and cultural studies, in Trude Fonneland's case, and in archaeology for Tiina Äikäs, enable us to approach the materialities of religion using interviews, participatory observations, and material culture. Archaeologists have been interested in the materiality of rituals for some time. Timothy Insoll states in *The Oxford Handbook of the Archaeology of Ritual and Religion* that "[a] 'turn' is also increasingly evident whereby serious consideration is beginning to be given to the materiality of ritual and religions" (Insoll 2011: 1). Simultaneously, there has also been increasing interest among archaeologists to document and study the material remains of contemporary times (e.g., Lucas & Buchli 2001; Harrison & Schofield 2010; Holtorf & Piccini 2011). In addition, the contemporary deposits at ritual sites have been studied from an archaeological perspective, for example, the New Age deposits in Chaco Canyon, New Mexico (Finn 1997); Pagan groups' uses of prehistoric sites in Britain (Blain & Wallis 2007; Houlbrook 2022), as well as in Finland, Norway, and Estonia (Äikäs & Spangen 2016; Jonuks & Äikäs 2019); and the use of coin-trees, where coins are pressed into trees and logs in exchange for a wish or luck (Houlbrook 2018, 2022). Archaeological studies are often concerned with offerings and deposits where the practices most often give birth to archaeological material. Here we study the contemporary material culture of offerings as well as of other kinds of spiritual practices.

Shamanism in General and Saami Shamanism in Particular[2]

The Western world's fascination with shamanism is by no means a recent phenomenon. The historical background has been meticulously documented by, among others, Ronald Hutton (2001), Kocku von Stuckrad (2003), and Andrei Znamenski (2007). The highlighting of shamanism as a universal

---

[2] The Saami people are the Indigenous people inhabiting northern Fennoscandia, which today encompasses parts of Sweden, Norway, Finland, and the Kola Peninsula of Russia. In Norway, the Saami are recognized under the international conventions of Indigenous people and are the northernmost Indigenous people of Europe. Their livelihood has traditionally been based on different types of hunting, fishing, gathering, husbandry, and agriculture, with considerable variation between different Saami groups. When using Saami concepts such as *sieidi* and *noaidi*, we follow the North Saami orthography if not otherwise mentioned. The word Saami itself has been written in different forms, including Saami, Sami, and Sámi. We have chosen to use Saami but in direct citations Sami and Sámi are also used. Translations from Norwegian and Finnish are our own if not otherwise mentioned.

phenomenon was inspired by the English translation of *Shamanism: Archaic Techniques of Ecstasy*, by Romanian historian of religion Mircea Eliade (1964). Eliade and his groundbreaking work have influenced not only the study but also the practice of shamanism (Wallis 2003). In addition, anthropologist Carlos Castaneda's experiential novel, *The Teachings of Don Juan: A Yaqui Way of Knowledge* (1968), served as an inspiration for numerous spiritual seekers. In the 1960s the so-called New Age movement turned to shamanism as a major inspiration and source for its worldview, and in the early 1970s shamanism emerged as a global category and phenomenon, with shamans in many parts of the world sharing common practices, rituals, and a nature-oriented worldview and lifestyle. As Thomas Karl Alberts argues:

> Since the 1970s, several constellations of interests and values have given a new prominence to shamanic religiosities, stimulated new proliferation and intensifications of shamanism discourse, and variously deepened and extended shamanism's entanglements in domains of knowledge and practice in which it was previously less prominent. (Alberts 2015: 2)

Michael Harner must be addressed as a major player when it comes to developing Eliadean shamanism into a spiritual path for everyone and creating mystical states that are achievable in a suburban living room or a New Age workshop (Harvey 2010; Sidky 2010). In 1979, Harner founded the Center for Shamanic Studies, a nonprofit organization that he renamed in 1987 as the Foundation for Shamanic Studies (FSS). Here he developed core shamanism, a system designed for Westerners to apply shamanism and shamanic healing successfully to their daily lives.[3] The FSS has three primary aims: preservation of shamanic cultures and wisdom around the world; study of the original shamanic peoples and their traditions; and teaching shamanic knowledge for the benefit of the planet. Several critics claim that Harner and his followers' use of the term shamanism is a cultural appropriation of non-Western practices by middle class "white" people who have distanced themselves from their own history (see Kehoe 2000: 3; Hutton 2001; Znamenski 2007). Even though Harner's theory of core shamanism claims that shamanism is not bound to any specific cultural group or perspective but is particularly "intended for Westerners to reacquire access to their rightful spiritual heritage,"[4] Harner's concept at the same time contributes to the construction of shamanism as "something out there," with Indigenous practitioners being the authentic shamans.

Contemporary shamanism has, more or less due to Harner's teaching, emerged as diverse religious practices used by a variety of actors all over the

---

[3] www.shamanism.org/fssinfo/index.html.

[4] See www.shamanism.org/workshops/coreshamanism.html.

world for various reasons and from different points of departure (Alberts 2018; Fonneland 2017; Kraft 2022). Within this global shamanic fellowship, diversity is the most prominent feature, and shamanism is therefore not describable as a uniform tendency on a global scale. Diversity is displayed in terms of the various traditions that the practitioners choose to follow and revive, in terms of practices, politics, values, and where it is all taking place. What this means is that studies of the dynamics of shamanic entrepreneurships and materialities in one particular place are not necessarily directly transferable to other local contexts. Although the United States can be described as the cradle of modern shamanism, the spread of shamanic religious practices and ideas to other habitats is not a uniform process but rather involves adaptations to local cultural and political climates.

In previous studies, Fonneland traced the history of the process of giving shamanism an Indigenous Saami flavor to Saami author and journalist Ailo Gaup (1944–2014), who is considered the first Saami shaman in Norway (see Fonneland 2010, 2017a). Gaup's story reveals both a strong influence from Harner's core shamanism and a strong desire to bring forth Saami religious traditions as a basis for religious practice in contemporary society (see Gaup 2005). In a memorial to Ailo Gaup at the FSS website the strong bond between Gaup and Harner is emphasized:

> Ailo had been a student of Michael Harner and played an important role in the restoration of Sami shamanism in Norway. He was a renowned poet, author, and a nephew of the famous Sami shaman, Mikkel Gaup. Just before Ailo became ill, he published Michael's *Cave and Cosmos* in Norwegian. Those who participated in Foundation courses with him will fondly remember his laughter and humor. [5]

While Harner's seminal *The Way of the Shaman*, published in 1980, does not mention Indigenous people, his FSS establishes a strong bond between core shamanism and Indigenous people. It pursues the idea that Indigenous forms of nature spirituality can be adapted to the inclinations and needs of those seeking alternative forms of enlightenment (see Alberts 2015: 131). This shift towards indigenism, and in particular towards Saami Indigenous traditions, is strongly reflected in the development of shamanism in Nordic countries.[6]

---

[5] https://shamanism.org/news/2014/page/2/.

[6] A rune-singer and an instructor of traditions, Eero Peltonen (2021) describes in the article "Rumpuystäväni" (My drum friend) how the new wave of shamanism arrived in Finland in the early 1980s as Michael Harner and anthropologist Heimo Lappalainen taught a course on shamanism at the University of Helsinki. According to Peltonen, a wider interest was raised by a play, *Eeli, shamaani* (Eeli, a shaman), performed at the Kajaani City theater in 1985, which offered a recounting of Elias Lönnrot, collector of the Finnish national epoch *Kalevala*. Hence,

Harner-style shamanism reached the Nordic region during the 1970s, along with New Age and occult impulses. During the first ten years, the shamanic movement was more or less a copy of the system developed by Harner in the United States. Similarly, the broader New Age scene differed little from its equivalent in the United States (Andreassen & Fonneland 2002). However, over the course of the first five years of the new millennium, the situation gradually changed (Fonneland & Kraft 2013). From this period forward, professional shamans were depicted as representing an ancient Saami sha-manic tradition (Christensen 2005), while the Nordic New Age scene was increasingly filled with Saami shamans, symbols, and traditions, along with a new focus on local- and place-specific characteristics unique to the northern region, particularly in terms of domestic geography (Fonneland 2010). Contemporary Saami shamanism has become a core subject within the wider field of shamanism in Nordic countries.

In Nordic countries, the term shaman has also become an umbrella term for the Saami *noaidi* (a north Saami term for a Saami Indigenous religious special-ist), similar to cases of religious specialists among people referred to as "Indigenous," more or less regardless of their particular expertise and practices. However, the noaidi has not always been perceived as a shaman. As David Chidester points out, the shaman is a religious specialist initially identified in Siberia, then colonized by Russia, and later adopted by a global arena (Chidester 2018: xi). In other words, the term shaman started its journey in European conceptualizations of Evenki practices in the late seventeenth century before extending beyond Siberia, and the concept has been expanding in space and time ever since.

Konsta Kaikkonen, in his doctoral dissertation, "Contextualising Descriptions of Noaidevuohta: Saami Ritual Specialists in Texts Written until 1871" (2020), points out that the discourse of "Saami shamanism" entered the academic world through the paradigm of comparative mythology as adopted by Finnish ethnographer and linguist Matthias Alexander Castrén in the 1840s. Building on Castrén's theories and ideas, in 1871 Norwegian linguist Jens A. Friis introduced this discourse into the up-and-coming field of "lappology." The concept of the shaman, in other words, is an example of the complexities often involved in translation processes over time and across space (see Znamenski 2007; Rydving 2011; Johnson & Kraft 2017; Nikanorova 2022). These translation processes were never equitable and neutral, and they fed colonial perceptions, exotification, and othering. When it comes to the types

---

Kalevalaic tradition has been connected to contemporary shamanism in Finland from the very beginning, as have influences from Harner.

of translation processes to which the terms shaman and shamanism have been subjected, it is important to keep in mind what James Clifford has highlighted with regard to the concept of translation: "Translation is not transmission. . . . Cultural translation is always uneven, always betrayed. But this very interference and lack of smoothness is a source of new meanings, of historical traction" (Clifford 2013: 48–9).

Climate: The North as a Spiritual Geography

Shamanic materialities produce religious spaces that address specific material conditions and shifting social networks. Through the drum, the sacred place, the power animal, and the mushroom, local sites take shape as spiritual geographies and centers. These spiritual geographies reveal the dwellings and crossings (Tweed 2006) of people, symbols, and rituals. The spiritual geography develops in dialogue with contemporary narratives about the north as a resource, symbolically, economically, climatically, and culturally. These ways of communicating the north are in sharp contrast to the perception of the north only a decade ago as "backward and less developed" in terms of lifestyle, education level, work opportunities, economy, and culture (see Grønaas et al. 1948).

The role of Saami as the Indigenous people of Northern Fennoscandia – Norway, Sweden, Finland, and the Kola Peninsula in Russia – raises ethical considerations with regard to the use of Saami cultural elements (Äikäs & Salmi 2019; Mathisen 2020). There have traditionally been different Saami cultures and languages. Moreover, today the Saami people have different cultures and histories, as well as being subject to different laws and regulations by nation-states despite their shared Indigenous identity. Despite being "one people," not all Saami enjoy the same rights or representation across the four nation-states due to these different national and cultural influences (Josefsen & Skogerbø 2021; Lilleslåtten 2021). Norway is the only Nordic country to have ratified ILO Convention No. 169 (Indigenous and Tribal Peoples Convention), which states that Indigenous people require "special measures, which promote the social and economic rights of the peoples concerned and protect their spiritual and cultural values."[7] These types of regulations also affect how shamanic materialities are approached and activated.

In other words, Saami shamanism exemplifies the importance of national frameworks and regulations with respect to religious developments in this case, and also in the sense of legal definitions regarding what constitutes a religion (see Gilhus & Kraft 2019: 15). The external forces of governmental laws and

---

[7] www.ilo.org/dyn/normlex/en/f?p=NORMLEXPUB:55:0::NO::P55_TYPE,P55_LANG, P55_DOCUMENT,P55_NODE:REV,en,C169,/Document.

regulations have direct consequences for the design and maneuverability of shamanistic groups. A law on religious freedom has been enshrined in Finland since 1923 and in Norway since 1964, which has also made it possible for groups without any affiliation to the Church of Norway, the Evangelical Lutheran Church of Finland, or the Orthodox Church of Finland to be classified legally as religious communities. In Finland, registered religious associations can perform legally valid marriage ceremonies and teach their respective religions in elementary schools and high schools if at least three pupils require it (see Taira 2010). In Norway, an approved religious community may perform ceremonies such as initiations, weddings, and funerals. While no country provides the same level of financial support for religious communities, registered religious communities receive similar public subsidies per member, as does the Norwegian Church (see Askeland 2011). The presence of a high number of "organized groups" distinguishes the shamanic topography in Norway from its Nordic neighbors (Gilhus & Kraft 2017: 11). As Gilhus and Kraft (2017: 11) argue, this might be due to the Protestant Church's strong position, whereby the church functions as a model for how religion should be shaped and organized. Norway is also the only Nordic country in which a shamanistic group has received recognition as an official religion (see Fonneland 2015). In Finland, Karhun kansa was the first pagan community to gain the status of a registered religious community in 2013. The Shamaaniseura (Shaman Association) is recognized not as a religion but rather as a religiously, politically, and ideologically independent organization, as stated on its website (Shamaaniseurary 2022, usein-kysytyt-kysymykset).

What this tells us is that shamanic materialities are not neutral but entangled in and in dialogue with local social and political trends and tensions (see also Strmiska 2018: 10). An examination of the local setting, climate, and local politics are thus important in order to understand precisely the domestic traits of shamanism.

Since the start of the twenty-first century, several researchers have claimed that shamanism is one of the fastest growing religions in the Western world (Wallis 2003: 140; Partridge 2004: 47). This growth is reflected in the Nordic countries in both secular and religious arenas. Various shamanic festivals, each with its own particular content and scope, have recently emerged (see Fonneland 2015a). New shamanic denominations are being constructed (see Fonneland 2015b), and a growing corpus of shamans are offering their services and products to the public. Furthermore, shamanism and articulations of Saami religion are being expressed in secular arenas like the tourism industry, media, films, products for sale and consumption, and the education system (see Christensen 2013; Äikäs 2019; Andreassen & Olsen 2020; Fonneland 2020; Kalvig 2020; Mathisen 2020). Shamanism has also been recently activated in various forms of political activism, often with a spotlight on the environment and saving the planet (see Kraft 2020). Saami shamanism therefore caters to not only spiritual needs but also the more mundane needs of the tourist trade, place branding, and entertainment, as well as for Saami nation building and the ethno-political field of Indigenous revival.

Shamanism in Nordic countries takes shape through the selection and inter-pretation of the "local" and the "traditional," and through the activation of different events, practices, and materialities that are highlighted as particularly meaningful for shamanic practitioners. Authenticity is here tied to distant times and places, to a past not yet touched by the detrimental influence of civilization, and to an authentic, organic Nordic culture living on in the guise of Christianity (see also Gregorius 2008: 132). Embedded in this quest for a Nordic past, a critique of civilization – a form of anti-modernism and anti-urbanism – can be traced. This quest and narrative also underpin and develop discourse about Indigenous religion by presenting Saami cultures as spiritual, close to nature, in balance with the natural elements, and associated with ancient traditions. In this Element, we use the connection of shamanism to Saami religions as a starting point but also scrutinize how shamanism has moved into other spiritual and even popular culture contexts.

Theoretical Framework

In this Element, we take the material turn as inspiration to look into the relations between things and humans – how things play an important role in shaping shamanic entrepreneurships in contemporary Nordic countries and how sha-manism happens in material culture. "Thinking through things" reveals how things create people as much as people create things. As Daniel Miller states:

> We cannot comprehend anything, including ourselves, except as a form. . . . We cannot know who we are. Or become what we are, except by looking in a material mirror, which is the historical world created by those who lived before us. This world confronts us as material culture and continues to evolve through us. (Miller 2005: 8)

The diverse and complex contemporary expressions of shamanic materialities can be described as processes of religion-making. Religion-making, according to a model developed by Markus Dressler and Arvind Mandair (2011), sheds light on the manifold layers of agency in religionization processes.[8] In their model,

---

[8] Dressler and Mandair draw on social constructivist and postcolonial approaches and are inspired by the studies of Edward Said (1978), Jonathan Z. Smith (1988), Talal Asad (1993, 2003), and Tomoko Masuzawa (2005).

Dressler and Mandair put forward three different levels of religion-making that shed light on multiple layers of agency in religionization processes:

> (1) religion-making from above, that is as a strategy from a position of power, where religion becomes an instrument of governmentality, a means to legitimize certain politics and positions of power; (2) religion-making from below, that is, as a politics where particular social groups in a subordinate position draw on a religionist discourse to re-establish their identities as legitimate social formations distinguishable from other social formations through tropes of religious difference and/ or claims for certain rights; and (3) religion-making from (a pretended) outside, that is, scholarly discourses on religion that provide legitimacy to the first two processes of religion-making by systematizing and thus normalizing the religious/secular binary and its derivates. (Dressler & Mandair 2011: 21)

An additional arena of religion-making was added by Dressler in "Modes of Religionization: A Constructivist Approach to Secularity" – namely what he refers to as religion-making in cultural encounters, "and the translations and negotiations of new and old concepts and practices that they engender" (Dressler 2019: 13). Dressler and Mandair are concerned with the linkages between these major dimensions and how some or all of them can be intertwined. They point out that religion-making from below forms a dialectical relationship with religion-making from above, and that attention needs to be given to the "more complex dynamics of agency in the adaptation of these discourses in non-Western vernacular languages" (Dressler & Mandair 2011: 22). They argue, with reference to Charles Hallisey's concept of intercultural mimesis, that:

> We need to think the appropriation of the Western discourses of religion and the secular in a manner that does not reduce local actors to the role of passive objects but instead focuses on "local productions of meaning," that is, the agency of locals in the encounter with Orientalist knowledge. (Dressler & Mandair 2011: 22)

Religion-making can also be connected to history-making when there is an experienced connection with religious traditions of the past. Brian Roberts, for instance, describes how history-making can be constructed of public and private, individual and group narratives (2004: 91). Different people, groups, and media create various stories of the past, which can serve present purposes and influence each other. Hence, history-making can be seen as a social process (Kalela 2013).[9] When people's experiences of the past, and interactions with the relics of the past, become part of history-making, the process can be seen as highly embodied. In recent decades, embodiment, bodily practice, and

---

[9] History-making can also be seen in the context of traditionalization discussed in Section 3.

performance have become a main focus of rituals and religion (Bell 1992; Insoll 2009; Salmi et al. 2011; Mitchell 2018). The body is approached "as a site of lived experience, a social body, and site of embodied agency" (Joyce 2005: 139). Bodily experience is seen as an important part of rituals and religion, as rituals are experienced with both one's body and all senses and emotions (Insoll 2009: 303). As Jon P. Mitchell observes:

> Embodiment figures the body as both locus and conduit of embodied religion; the subject, rather than object, of religious process. The concern is therefore less with religious regulation of the body, or the body as symbolic represen-tation of religious meaning, than with the various ways in which religion is enacted, performed, embodied. (Mitchell 2018: 1)

Äikäs and Ikäheimo have shown how people can bring the past into the present through interaction and bodily engagement (Ikäheimo & Äikäs 2017). Here the historicity of the relic is not as important as the possibility for bodily engagement with it.

In all of the preceding contexts mentioned, indigeneity and "Indigenous religion" are approached as cultural capital (Bourdieu 1973). For a variety of reasons, a range of diverse actors view Indigenous spirituality as something that is worth pursuing, owning, and consuming. This has led to controversies and to questions about appropriation. Colonialism is not just about territorial claims, economic strategies, and racial ideologies; it also involves the appropriation of material culture (Naum & Nordin 2013; Äikäs & Salmi 2019).

Religion, Worldview, and Way of Life

The concept of religion is and has been imbued with varying connotations and values in different societies and contexts. In the shamans' descriptions, the word religion is absent. Shamanic praxeology, ontology, and cosmology are described here in broad rubrics as ancient techniques and as holistic ways of life in close contact with and respect for nature. In addition, their statements can be said to exhibit what Heelas termed "unmediated individualism" (1996: 21) by placing a high value on individual freedom and autonomy and revealing a suspicion towards institutional structures. Contrary to religion, shamanism is approached as a worldview or way of life, one that is closely linked to an individual practitioner's own inner guidance. As Ann Taves and Michael Kinsella (2018) underline: "To govern a way of life, a worldview does not necessarily have to be highly elaborated or rationalized or even explicitly articulated. It may be expressed in practice (enacted), represented (in objects), articulated (in speech), recounted (in story), and textualized (in writing)."[10]

---

[10] See www.mdpi.com/journal/religions/special_issues/-ethnographies, accessed January 8, 2022.

As such, the terms worldview and way of life both embrace the individual aspect that the shamans emphasize. Rather than an organized movement with identifiable doctrines, practices, and leaders, shamanism in Nordic countries is complex, multifaceted, and loosely organized. It shows how local pasts, places, and characters are woven into global discourses on shamanism and how, in this developing fabric, new forms of practices and worldviews are taking shape.

Shamans use new technologies to reroute spiritual and cultural connections. The Internet is an important site of shamanic mobilization through which shamanistic materialities can be presented and utilized. With members and devotees of shamanism spread across the globe, the Internet has become a key component in the organization and marketing of shamanistic materialities, in large part because it allows individuals in entirely different locations to communicate with each other and for pictures and information to be disseminated more easily. The Internet has thus played an important role in popularizing materialities and making them accessible everywhere (Pike 2004: 18; Kuparikettu & Saure 2021)

Every shamanic organization, and each individual entrepreneur, has designed their own website to serve as a guide for the uninitiated who are browsing for information on shamanism and to distribute information about courses, events, and products. In addition, social media and online forums remain important arenas in which people with an interest in shamanism can keep in touch with others who share their spiritual concerns. Particularly during a time and in a world characterized by the coronavirus, social media like Facebook have become arenas for shamans to develop and share materialities and narratives that articulate indigeneity and claims of sacredness, often in opposition to scientific perspective and practices, as well as salient spaces for fieldwork.

Method and Structure

Shamanistic materialities relate to a Saami Indigenous spirituality and the Saami past through celebration of pop-up as well as seasonal rituals, festivals, courses, shamanic entrepreneurships, tourism events, and cultural politics. These materialities are not inauthentic expressions that circulate visions of a Saami past but rather a vibrant form of contemporary religiosity, drawing on a range of historical, cultural, and archaeological resources. As Stuart Hall contends:

> Everywhere, cultural identities are emerging which are not fixed, but poised, in transition, between different positions; which draw on different cultural traditions at the same time; and which are the product of those complicated crossovers and cultural mixes which are increasingly common in a globalized world. (Hall 1992: 310)

Inspired by Meredith B. McGuire's *Lived Religion* (2008), the authors of this Element investigate how shamanistic materialities are enacted in people's everyday lives – not how they are defined by religion scholars and organizations – in hope of unveiling a more nuanced understanding of contemporary shamanism. Such a study allows us to see how theory is put into practice, how materiality impacts different aspects of life, and the ways in which worldview must affect, and be expressed in, everyday life (Bowman & Valk 2012: 2). Careful observation of process and practice and the significance of individual creativity and instrumentality in relation to tradition remain crucial when trying to comprehend culture and do justice to "religion as it is lived" (Primiano 1995: 44).

Religion as it is lived can only be properly understood through fieldwork. This Element draws on interviews with a variety of practitioners of shamanism in Norway and Finland, as well as on participant observation at ceremonies, rituals, fairs, and festivals. We have also interviewed people who produce shamanistic materiality but whose own spirituality is not necessarily related to shamanism. Some of the interviewees expressed a wish to stay anonymous. We are aware we can only get partial views through interviews and fieldwork, but we also know that we can work to expand our outlook. A constant awareness of our limited access to other experiences makes us agree with James Clifford's statement that "listening for histories" is now more important than "telling it like it is" (Clifford 2013: 23–4).

One of the key sources for data from Finland is a web survey that Äikäs conducted together with Tõnnu Jonuks (Estonian Literary Museum) in November–December 2021. The survey was circulated via the email lists and Facebook groups of various contemporary pagan groups in Finland and Estonia. It received 119 responses, most of them from Finland. The contemporary pagan groups were not all directly linked to shamanism, but since many of the participants identified themselves as part of several groups, we were also able to contact people whose spirituality included shamanism. Fifteen of the participants stated that they relate to shamanism. Those identifying themselves as following shamanism added other groups as well, most often Suomalainen muinaisusko (Finnish paganism) or nature-centered spirituality (67 percent each).

In addition to interviews, participant observations, and the web survey, we also used material culture as a source. Äikäs has documented contemporary deposits at Saami sacred places in Finland and Norway since 2008 (e.g., Äikäs 2015; Äikäs & Spangen 2016). While attending shamanistic events, she has also paid close attention to the material culture evident at the gatherings.

The sections in this Element are based on specific case studies, exploring the uses and interpretations of shamanism in varying contexts. As our work is based on our encounters with both people and materiality, we have deemed it important to make these personal encounters visible in the text. Hence, there are different narrators in different sections using the first tense verb form. Fonneland is the narrator of Sections 1 and 4, and Äikäs of Sections 2 and 3. We have nevertheless coauthored all the sections.

In the first section, we explore the role of drums within the field of contemporary shamanism. The drum reveals how a material cultural artifact has different "lives" and applications as an identity marker, as well as how it is disseminated widely and adapted to very different cultural environments and functions. In the second section, we scrutinize Saami sacred places as sites of personal, communal, and organized offering rituals. We explore how both real and imagined pasts are part of the ways people interact with the sites and how these interactions again affect the history-making at the sites. In Section 3, power animals are discussed in various contexts – from shamanistic festivals to video games and symbols in clothing. Power animals are performed through multiple embodied practices such as dance, wearing ornaments, and meditation, and in the practices, questions of spirituality, identity, and material presentations are intertwined. Section 4 takes its starting point in the mushroom known as chaga, the use of which has, over the last ten years, become apparent in several shamanistic environments in the Nordic countries in mythology, medicine, economics, and tourism as well as a producer of sacred space and a commodity for personal consumption and enjoyment.

Our investigations of the drums, sacred places, power animals, and chaga show how shamanic materialities are closely linked to circulations and dynamics of categories and discourses and deeply entangled in processes of religion- and history-making.

1 Shaman Drums: Contemporary Tools for Religion-Making

When I, Trude Fonneland, as a PhD student in 2006 visited shaman Ailo Gaup in his home at Hovseter in Oslo, he was clear about one thing. He was not satisfied with the frame for my PhD thesis. Gaup wished what he had found was a much more relevant and interesting research topic, with more research questions devoted to exploring it, namely the study of the sound waves and vibrations of the shaman drums. He saw the drum as the center of his shamanic practices and related to the drum as the main tool for entering shamanic states of consciousness.

As a folklorist and cultural researcher, I could not accommodate Gaup's request. The study of vibrations was far beyond my area of expertise. But the meeting with Gaup left no doubt about his view of the drum as a powerful tool for interaction with spiritual powers. In 1988, Gaup published a novel, *Trommereisen* (*The Drum Journey*), that conveys a story about a male character, Jon, who starts to dream about a bowl drum (goavddis) – an instrument known from northern Saami areas and decorated with the symbol of the sun and other Saami emblems – that floats in a sea of flames. Jon's dreams about the burning drum become a starting point for a personal spiritual journey into the world of his Saami ancestors. *The Shaman Zone* (2005), which Gaup published seven years later, reveals that the novel was in fact a story about Gaup's own personal experiences. He writes:

> The drums of the tribe began to call when I reached a mature age. It happened through dreams. I started to dream about a Sámi shaman drum. . . . It floated on a sea of fire. The dream came to me several times. I knew I had to save the drum from burning up. Eventually, I understood that the dream was a mythological message because the drum did not catch fire where it lay in the flaming sea. . . . My call as a shaman consisted of finding the knowledge held by the drums. (Gaup 2005: 40)

In the search for his own Saami identity and for the traces of the Saami bowl drum, Gaup returned to Guovdageaidnu (Kautokeino) in the mid-1970s. But in Guovdageaidnu and in the nearby Saami communities, the drums had been lost since the entry of missionaries into the society. At the beginning of the eighteenth century, the organized mission of the Danish–Norwegian state, inspired by pietism – the Mission Collegium – was established and led by Thomas von Westen (1682–1727). These missionary processes were diverse and dramatic, involving not only missions but also events such as so-called witch trials, international political conflicts, and even war (see Willumsen 2010; Hansen & Olsen 2014; Storm 2014; Hagen 2015).

The missionaries managed to disrupt traditional Saami religion as a comprehensive religious system through persecution and punishment of people who used ritual drums, through collection and destruction of ritual drums, destruction of sacred sites (*sieiddit*), and building of churches (see Hansen & Olsen 2014; Storm 2014; Hagen 2015). During the seventeenth and eighteenth centuries, hundreds, perhaps thousands, of drums vanished over a period of about 100 years. The drums were ripped, smashed, burned in bonfires, forcibly rounded up by missionaries, or hidden in the mountains to be later found and presented to collectors or museums. In short, there was a process of taking drums and giving Bibles.[11]

---

[11] Similarly, sacred places were destroyed, desecrated, and left unused, thereby losing their power. It has been suggested that these actions against sacred places only led some people to use more personal sites instead of communal, well-known sacred sites (Rydving 1993: 65–6, 101–2).

Gaup's dream about the bowl drum on a sea of flames can be seen as a symbol of these violent acts. But the fact that the drum in the dream did not give in to the flames gave him hope that by returning home to his birth land and looking for traces of the old Saami religion, some of the Saami mythology could be located, rescued, and rebuilt.

As I have elaborated in *Contemporary Shamanisms in Norway* (Fonneland 2017a), however, what Gaup found in Finnmark that could be related to the practice of the old Saami religion had no apparent connection to the *goavddis*, the Saami bowl drum for which he was searching. At the Tourist Hotel in Guovdageaidnu, Gaup met a Chilean refugee, Ernesto, who practiced drum journeys and was willing to teach him the art. This was also how Gaup's first ritual visit to the spirit world of his ancestors came about, by way of Chilean traditions, accompanied by an African djembe drum (Gaup 2005: 86–98). Gaup comments: "And so it happened that I, who had traveled around the Polar Circle to find a Sámi noaidi to learn from, wound up in an attic in Oslo with a half-breed Indian carrying a djembe drum. I thought it was a good mix of cultural elements" (Gaup 2005: 95).

Shortly after this experience, Gaup was contacted by shaman Michael Harner, widely acknowledged as the world's foremost authority on shamanism, and he decided to leave for Esalen, to step onto Harner's path of core shamanism.

The Construction of the Drum and Drum Journey as Primary Elements of Shamanism

As a graduate student of anthropology, Michael Harner spent considerable time with different Indigenous people in the Ecuadorian and Peruvian Amazon. In 1963 he defended his doctoral dissertation, "Machetes, Shotguns, and Society: An Inquiry into the Social Impact of Technological Change among the Jivaro Indians." Inspired by his studies, Harner changed the course of his life by starting on the shamanic path, and in 1979 he founded the Center for Shamanic Studies in Norwalk, Connecticut. A year later, based on experiences from his fieldwork, he published *The Way of the Shaman* (1980), which has been foundational in the development and popularization of core shamanism as a path of personal development for adherents. Today, the book has the status of one of the foremost shamans' textbooks and serves as a guide that demonstrates how to proceed step-by-step on the path of the shaman. Gaup has on several occasions referred to this book as his main inspiration and as a "dharma," or guide, for contemporary shamans. In *The Shamanic Zone* he writes:

> *The Way of the Shaman* is for me a book that handles the principles and what is necessary to learn in order to get personal experience. Thus, it gives the impression of being a sacred scripture, or shamanic dharma. I have read the

book several times and each time it gives me new insights. It is a modern classic and will remain a milestone, not just for shamans, but also as a work that contributed to a shift in the very spirit of this time. (Gaup 2005: 224)

Through Harner's courses and publications, core shamanism grew into the most popular form of contemporary shamanism. Harner describes core shamanism as an attempt to unite all the world's shaman traditions and claims that it is possible to link the various shamanistic traditions together into a whole without violating the individual tradition.

Within core shamanism the drum acts as an ultimate focusing device and meditation vessel, transporting the shaman's spirit into non-ordinary realities. The drum journey is described by Harner (1980) as a technique in which one changes consciousness at will through using a drum. This journey travels to other realities in the upper and lower world, where beings called spirits can bring guidance, strength, and advice. Harner provides instructions for how the drum should be used for traveling into the lower or upper world; this instruction has developed into a standard that is practiced by shamans when performing drum journeys in Nordic countries as well.[12]

In other words, the drum is a tool of power that, according to Harner, should be treated with restraint and respect. It is approached as a living being with the ability to carry the shamanic practitioner to the source of spiritual wisdom. One of the stated missions of the Foundation for Shamanic Studies (FSS) is to help to revive and preserve Indigenous shamanic knowledge in areas where, according to the FSS, these traditions have been lost or are threatened. This includes, not least, reviving what the FSS lists as the main tool for shamanic practices, the drum. Hearing that the drum had disappeared among the Saami, Harner wanted to see for himself, and at the beginning of the 1980s he visited Sápmi[13] twice to gain knowledge about Saami culture and religion. Searching for traces of Saami shamanism, he visited Ailo Gaup's uncle, the Saami Mikkel Gaup, a well-known "wise man" in Norway as well as in a broader Scandinavian context, bearing the nicknames "Miracle Mikkel" and "Healing Fox." Harner describes this meeting in *Cave and Cosmos* (2013) as one of the high points in his anthropological fieldwork. He points out that Mikkel Gaup did not use the drum journey or even the drum in his healing, and that most of the practices connected with the drum had disappeared among the Saami. Looking back, Harner identifies a turning point regarding the use of the drum in this region: "drum journeying is now slowly starting to return there, partly because of help

---

[12] See https://shamanism.org/fssinfo/index.html.

[13] Sápmi is the North Saami name for the Saami's historical settlement area and extends across four nation-states, encompassing parts of Norway, Sweden, Finland, and the Kola Peninsula of Russia.

from the FSS and my former students, one of them a Sámi" (Harner 2013: 131). He sees his visit as an important catalyst that paved the way for new religious ideas to change prevailing local practices and to revive the drum as a tool in religious rituals. The Saami student that Harner mentions as an important contributor who ensured that shamanism and the drum got a foothold in Sápmi is Ailo Gaup, recognized as the founder of the Norwegian shamanic movement.

The Return of Drums

Upon the completion of his training in California in the 1980s, Gaup returned from Esalen with a backpack full of ideas and inspirations about core shamanism, drums, and drum journeys, propelled by Harner's teaching. At this time in the Nordic countries, drums had not yet been established as powerful symbols and were seldom highlighted as markers of Saaminess. Nor had shamanism, as a global new religious trend, developed full-grown networks. These types of developments supplemented shamanic catalysts such as Ailo Gaup and Arthur Sørenssen in Norway, Jørgen Eriksson in Sweden, Anette Høst and Jonathan Horwitz in Denmark, and Johannes Setälä in Finland. What many of these shamanic pioneers have in common is that they honor Michael Harner as one of their first human teachers. They share a common starting point in core shamanism but then start to reorient their shamanic practices and seek inspiration from local religious traditions.

A central foundation for many of these founders is that the "old religions" never fully disappeared, and that some of these traditions can be restored and brought to life again in a contemporary context; that is, lost Indigenous and local religious traditions can be retrieved and connections made. The Finnish shaman Johannes Setälä reclaims his roots in the Finno-Ugric and Kalevala tradition (Aarnio n.d.), but he also draws inspiration from Saami history. In line with Harner, Setälä stresses the drums as the foremost medium for shamanistic travels and notes that the drum helps to connect with a long line of ancestors all the way to "the dawn of the births" (Setälä 2000: 6).[14]

Highlighting the drum as the most important symbol for shamanic practices runs parallel to, and is nourished by, other processes in Nordic society, such as Saami nation building that started in the early twentieth century (Zachariassen 2012)

---

[14] A cultural anthropologist and a practitioner of shamanism, Helena Karhu (2020) states that the popularity of shaman drums in Finland has grown in recent years. Even though there are no statistics, she estimates that several hundred drums are made annually. There are Finnish drum makers and drum courses, and people building their drums without guidance. There are also new forms of shamanistic material culture such as different instruments, talismans, shamans' staffs, clothes, and jewelry, which create new material heritage, according to Karhu.

and accelerated during the 1970s and 1980s (Bjørklund 2000). Referring to Krister Stoor (2016), Siv Ellen Kraft points out that on both the Swedish and Norwegian side of Sápmi, drums were stigmatized and not used as a symbol of Saaminess before the 1980s. She writes: "The shift to widespread presence and usage came after the turn of the century, and then through different forms, formats, and media, across fine art and popular culture and (to a more limited extent) in political domains" (Kraft 2022: 173). In a 2019 debate posted in the national newspaper *Aftenposten*, Aili Keskitalo, former president of the Sámediggi (Saami Parliament) in Norway, declared that the drum and the *ládjogahpir* (a traditional Saami women's hat) "are some of the strongest symbols of Sami cultural heritage deprived of us by force and exhibited to others."[15] Thus, the drums have detached themselves from a delimited religious context and been included in a broader field of cultural heritage – also reborn as heritage formation – and their public space has been expanded (see also Kraft 2022).

Within this complex and busy network of entrepreneurs, products, and theologies, the drum has become the most recognizable and most central of the Nordic shamanic artifacts and markers. Inspired by Harner, the drum took on a strong role in the Norwegian and Finnish shamanic environments beginning in the 1990s. Since then, it has circulated widely in the public space within the tourism sector, in art and popular culture, and in the entertainment industries (Kalvig 2020; Kraft 2020; Mathisen 2020).[16] In these settings, the drums are flexible and multivalent symbols of shamanic identities, but at the same time susceptible to many applications, interpretations, meanings, and values.

As Stein R. Mathisen (2020: 147) notes, drums "have moved from a dangerous noaidi's instrument of evil (in the eyes of colonizers and Christian missionaries) to a legitimate object in the souvenir shop." In Finland, the use of Saami motifs in the tourism industry, including symbols from drums and dolls wearing a traditional Saami costume, *gákti*, has a long tradition. Saami cultural elements especially became part of Christmas imagery in the 1980s when Christmas tourism to Lapland started (Jaakkola 2022). One of the most well-known companies is Lappituote, which offers shaman drums (Fi. *noitarumpu*) and products

---

[15] "Hornluen og trommen er derfor noen av de sterkeste symbolene på samisk kulturarv fratatt oss med makt og stilt ut for andre," www.aftenposten.no/meninger/debatt/i/70JR0B/vi-krever-retten-til-aa-eie-vaar-egen-historie-aili-keskitalo?form=MY01SV&OCID=MY01SV, accessed November 16, 2021.

[16] The Finnish folk metal band Korpiklaani, for instance, highlights the drum in several of their music videos. In the music video Rauta (The Iron), a man is drumming on a boulder (www.youtube.com/watch?v=PJwo6bMKBaw). In 2022, Finnish drum maker Juha Järvinen received media coverage as his drums were used in the production of the Viking movie *The Northman* (Leiwo 2022, www.iltalehti.fi/kotimaa/a/a248204d-04c0-4aab-94a5-16080d0b19a9).

Figure 1 Drums in a souvenir shop in Northern Norway. Photo by Tiina Äikäs, used by permission.

decorated with images of drums and drum symbols. These objects range from reindeer bells to fleece ponchos, and they have been produced for about thirty years.[17] As the only national Saami Parliament, the Saami Parliament in Finland issued "Responsible and Ethical Principles for Sustainable Sámi Tourism" (2018), which are guidelines for how Saami culture should be presented to tourists.[18] Despite these guidelines, the exploitation of Saami motifs, especially drum symbols, is still evident (Figures 1–3). They are used as decorative elements in souvenirs, clothes, food packages, and interior decoration (see also Joy 2019). Suvi Jaakkola (2022) states that when the symbols are taken from their original context, they are harnessed to create an image of mythical Lapland and exotic Saaminess (cf. Herva et al. 2020).[19] Still, reports like the one developed by the Saami Parliament in Finland are pressing means to promote sustainability and viability within the tourism industry in Sápmi.

Within the field of shamanism in Nordic countries, the drum is pressed into service for a variety of reasons. It is a ritual instrument, a tool for divination,

---

[17] www.lappituote.fi/etusivu/.   [18] https://samediggi.fi/saamelaismatkailu/en/.

[19] Some drum makers and shamans express concern for how the tourism industry has embraced and marketed the drums. The Saami craft artist Elli Maaret Helander, for instance, points out that she is not willing to produce or sell drums for souvenir shops because "she does not want to commercialize her work" (Joy 2014: 132; Joy 2018: 191).

Figure 2 Drums in a hotel restaurant in Northern Finland. Photo by Tiina Äikäs, used by permission.

Figure 3 Drum symbols on a bread package of "the flatbread of Lapland." Photo by Tiina Äikäs, used by permission.

a symbol for a shamanic identity, a marketing motif, a commodity, a map, a theology, and much more. The drum reveals how a material cultural artifact has different "lives" and applications as an identity marker, how it is disseminated widely and becomes adapted to very different cultural environments and functions. The remainder of this section looks closer at some of the drums' "lives" and how they are activated in shamanic contexts. Although my starting point is local, in contemporary society local expressions are in most cases seldom exclusively local but instead interact with global trends, often conveyed and constructed by contemporary mediascapes. Through the study of two Saami shamans, Eirik Myrhaug and Ronald Kvernmo, I explore how drums are used as tools in contemporary religion-making processes and how the drum in various forms of activism is featured as a transformative instrument.

Isogaisa Shaman Weekend

Shaman Ronald Kvernmo is the founder and leader of the Saami shaman festival Isogaisa, which has taken place in northern Norway every summer since 2010 (see Fonneland 2015, 2017a). When the coronavirus epidemic reached the country in March 2020, the prospects of arranging a larger, international gathering fell dramatically, and festival plans had to be rearranged. Kvernmo is a shaman entrepreneur with a footing in many different enterprises.[20] In addition to being a shaman, he is a tourist host offering dog sledding and spiritual northern lights experiences together with his wife, Beate Sandjord. Through the company Isogaisa Siida AS, Kvernmo also owns and runs his own alternative medicine company, developing and promoting chaga (a mushroom found on birch trees) as a natural supplement (see Section 4). Finally, he provides shamanic training, healing, and house cleansing.[21]

Kvernmo started his shaman career as an apprentice of Ailo Gaup and was particularly inspired by Gaup's approach to Saami shamanism. Kvernmo also studied the Saami religion and its sources at the Arctic University in Tromsø, where he was introduced to texts by missionaries and clergymen who in the seventeenth and eighteenth centuries wrote zealously about the "the Bible of the devil" (see Kildal 1910: 89), which they were intent on seizing and eradicating. Despite their bias, these texts are commonly referred to as the most relevant source material when studying Saami drums (see Rydving 1993, 1995).

In their attempt to remove and replace the local Saami religions with a pious Christian faith, the missionaries, through their confiscation of drums, destruction of sacred places, and inquisition of the Saami, systematized and

---

[20] "Spiritual entrepreneurs" provide a valuable insight into a key perspective on religion in contemporary society, namely how religion adapts to consumer culture and its values. Words like spirit, holism, deep values, and self-development, which are central in New Age thinking, appear here as key terms in the production of unique experiences for consumption (see Fonneland 2012). In using the term spiritual entrepreneur, our intention is to align with the growing cadre of scholars who are challenging the traditional dualistic view of religion and economics as separate and distinct (see Partridge 2004; Redden 2005; Kraft 2011). Through the development of a new religious landscape, the institutional forms of religion are being reshaped, and the religion economy is changing. The introduction of concepts with a spiritual connotation in some business circles is also in line with a wider tendency to put spirituality to work to enhance productivity (Aupers & Houtman 2006).

[21] https://newshop.isogaisa.org/.

theologized a Saami belief system. Scholars from the nineteenth century cat-
egorized this missionary construction as shamanism, a particular type of religion (see Kaikkonen 2020) that was associated with negative characteristics and
portrayed as primitive heresy until well into the twentieth century. The fact that
scholars classified Saami religions as shamanism, which consisted of central
elements such as the shaman and his tools – the drum and the drum hammer[22] –
is also the foundation for shamanism's "return" and the drum's status in
contemporary shamanism.

Kvernmo grew up at a time when he felt his Saami background was a stigma.
It was only when introduced to a shamanic environment that he chose to
emphasize his Saami identity (see Fonneland 2017a). The processes of constructing new Saami identities, shaped through contact with a global shamanistic environment, can be seen as an example of what Greg Johnson and Siv Ellen
Kraft (2017; with reference to Clifford 2013) highlight as a "dynamic of back" –
"how global indigeneity plays back home and is made local once again" (2017:
12). The process of becoming Saami and Indigenous through shamanistic
knowledge generation expresses a transformative renewal of attachments to
culture and place where the concept of Saami identity is expanded as well as
contested.

The Isogaisa Shaman Weekend was held in a *lávvu* (Saami tent) on the farm,
Kvernmo. Kvernmo is located in a small valley with only a few inhabitants,
a two-hour drive from Tromsø. It might seem risky to run a family business in
such a distant and sparsely populated area. Kvernmo's business shows that
small places that barely appear on the map can be crucial nodes for these types
of enterprises. Kvernmo represents an alternative geography, an attractive
destination in a tourist setting as well as in shamanic contexts, offering an
unusual experience and close-to-nature adventures far from the city's hustle.

Ronald Kvernmo starts the course by describing shamanism as the oldest
known method for healing, creativity, ecstasy, and power mobilization, and that
Indigenous people all over the world have their own "local" inspired forms of
shamanism. He also acknowledges that shaman–anthropologists such as Carlos
Castaneda and Michael Harner were important catalysts in terms of making
these techniques available to a Western audience. The growth of shamanism in
Nordic countries can be seen as a direct consequence of the efforts of Castaneda
and Harner. At the same time, Kvernmo presents himself as a guardian of Saami
traditions and emphasizes that his way into shamanism is connected to his roots
in Saami culture. He points out that his practice as a contemporary noaidi

---

[22] A T-shaped object often made of antler and used for drumming.

springs from symbols of the Saami religion that are woven into contemporary values and inspirations. One such inspiration is the drum.

Kvernmo's lecture for the shaman course begins with the most famous of these symbols, namely the drum that belonged to the Saami Poala-Ánde (Anders Poulsen), which was confiscated in 1691. The drum was central to the trial against Poala-Ánde that took place at the court session in Vadsø, February 9–10, 1692, which is considered the last of the great witchcraft trials in Finnmark. Even though his confession was given under pressure during interrogation, Poala-Ánde's story is important as a source of knowledge about Saami religions because his drum is preserved and because Poala-Ánde himself explained the meaning of the symbols during the trial (Rydving 1991; Hagen 2002; Willumsen 2022).[23] Poala-Ánde's drum became part of the Danish royal family's art collection before being transferred to Denmark's National Museum in 1849.

Poala-Ánde's drum, which was recently repatriated to the Sámiid Vuorká-Dávvirat, the Sámi collection in Kárasjohká, is painted with figures and the only known, preserved drum with five horizontal levels. Kvernmo compares this drum to drums from southern Saami areas, known as *gievrie* (frame drums), and drums from the area close to Rivták, his home area. Based on his interpretations of these drums, Kvernmo has developed his own personal drum, which is shaped like a bowl drum and decorated with drawings of Saami gods and goddesses, the symbol of the sun, nature elements, and Kvernmo's personal symbols, such as his power animals, a symbol for Internet Explorer, and a symbol for the road E6 – the European road that extends from the south of Sweden to the far north of Norway.

Kvernmo's drum reveals how a drum that was confiscated and a man who was killed while in custody for his beliefs in, and use of, the drum have become catalysts for contemporary shamanic religion-making. The drum that Kvernmo draws upon and lectures about serves as a frame for a contemporary Saami shamanic structure of spiritual beings, beliefs, and practices. Based on Kvernmo's studies of the sources, and his knowledge of scholars' interpretations of the drums and their symbols, a theologizing of contemporary Saami shamanism is taking place. Taking a starting point in the drums' structure, Kvernmo develops his own version of a contemporary Saami shamanic theology through his courses. On the drum's top level, he draws and highlights three Saami gods (Ibmil, Tiermes/Dierpmis, and Bieggaolmmái), the Saami goddess Mahtaráhkku, and a noaidi in the heavens (Figure 4). He points out that

---

[23] In addition to the court documents, the case is known through County Governor Hans H. Lilienskiold's book *Finmarchens beskrifuelsis* (ca. 1695).

Figure 4 Kvernmo teaches course participants about the drum and its symbols, August 2021. Photo by Trude Fonneland, used by permission.

the missionaries adopted the name Ibmil, and it became the Saami name of the Christian God. Tiermes, or Dierpmis in northern Saami, is presented as the thunder god and Bieggaolmmái as "the windman" who determines the wind's direction. Kvernmo describes Máhtaráhkku as the mother of the three goddesses Sáráhkku, Juksáhkku, and Uksáhkku and also refers to the goddess as Mother Earth. Over the years Mother Earth has become an established symbol in global shamanic contexts, especially connected to environmental concerns (Kraft 2020). Mahtaráhkku's encounter with Mother Earth reveals how global trends and politics are entwined in repeating processes of religion-making. The transformation has served to enlarge Mahtaráhkku's impacts, popularity, authority, and field of reference.

Two power animals are found on the drum's upper level – a bird and a reindeer. A symbol of the sun, *beaivi*, is placed in the drum's center, and the four sunbeams extend North, South, East, and West. Also, the goddesses Sáráhkku, Juksáhkku, and Uksáhkku are present along with symbols representing the home and the family, the mountains, and the woods.

The *lávvu*, where the course participants are gathered, takes shape as a classroom where a common understanding of Saami shamanism is developed. The participants listen, interrogate Kvernmo about the Saami gods' qualities, and make a copy of Kvernmo's drum in their notebooks. An ethnographic transformation of the source material, of Saami mythology, and oral narratives into a contemporary shamanic scriptural text with the drum as blackboard and frame occurs in the *lávvu*. The drum itself becomes a map of contemporary Saami shamanistic theology. At the same time, it functions as a bridging device – a trace – that opens continuity with the past where roots and routes are connected. It becomes a space where links are being made between *then* (and *there*) and *now* (and *here*).

The Drum as a Transformative Device

The second case study builds on conversations with shaman Eirik Myrhaug and his discussions and posts on various Facebook platforms, presentations at conferences, and his participation in diverse forms of activism. In these varying contexts the drum is highlighted as a symbolic device in struggles for the environment and the rights of nature, for a reconnection with Mother Earth, and for Indigenous rights and nature's rights. According to Myrhaug, the drum opens a transformative relationship between nature and humans and serves to restore the connection with Mother Earth and the recovery of Indigenous rights and knowledge systems.

Eirik Myrhaug, a Saami shaman, has been a central figure in the shamanic environment in Norway since the mid-1990s. Myrhaug grew up in Rivták (Gratangen), northern Norway in a Læstadian environment.[24] According to Myrhaug, in Rivták, parts of the old noaidi tradition survived, wrapped in the new Læstadian religion, especially through the Læstadian congregational rituals and prayer traditions (see Myrhaug 2018: 28). A theme of exile provides a picture of an Indigenous Saami religion that never fully disappeared but lived on under new designations. This theme has been enkindled by both shamans and scholars alike (see Paine 1965; Minde 2008; Solbakk 2008; Myrhaug 2018). An example of what Olav Hammer (2001: 85–200) has referred to as "the appeal to tradition," the theme of exile provides a historical base to the idea of an essential

---

[24] Læstadianism is a Lutheran church revival movement that was started by the Swedish priest Lars Levi Læstadius in Swedish Lapland. In the 1840s, the revival spread to Finland and northern Norway, and has since spread to several countries, including North America, England, Germany, Russia, and Estonia.

"Saaminess" across time and place, while at the same time adding authenticity to the current generations of Saami shamans to which Myrhaug belongs. Myrhaug's father and several other family members were trained in using prayers for healing of both humans and animals. Before his father died in the 1970s, Myrhaug inherited the prayer forms, but he was not yet ready to follow in his father's footsteps. Myrhaug trained as an engineer and worked for the Swedish construction company Skanska and the Norwegian Waterways and Electricity Company (Norges Vassdrag og Elektrisitetsvesen). Over the years, Myrhaug expressed growing interest in developing a new form of economy and published his first book, *The New Ecological Social Economy* (1982). The book was widely recognized and made Myrhaug a natural choice as head of the Norwegian Forum for Ecological Economy.

In 1981, Myrhaug took part in the Alta affair, known as a watershed in Saami political history affecting the Saamis' right to decide for themselves how to shape their culture and future (see Bjørklund 2013). Myrhaug was the leader of the second hunger strike against the damming of the Alta-Kautokeino river system – a case that was lost but at the same time laid the foundation for new Indigenous politics (see Myrhaug 2018: 28–33). Indigenous spiritual elements such as the drum were not part of the Alta protests (see Kraft 2022), as an Indigenous spiritual language had not yet been developed in Alta, nor in a larger Norwegian context. Still, the demonstrations sparked a spiritual interest in Myrhaug, and he remembered the healing formulas he had inherited. By this time in Norway, Ailo Gaup had established a series of courses with a core shamanistic focus that also took inspiration from Saami traditions. Myrhaug was introduced to Ailo Gaup in the late 1980s and describes him as the one "who brought the use of the shaman drum back to Norway, and that encouraged him to use the drum himself" (Myrhaug 2018: 28). Energized by Gaup, Myrhaug retrieved the healing formulas that his father had given him and developed a synthesis of traditional healing and modern shamanism.

Even though drums were long lost, and the Saami Indigenous religion considered taboo in Rivták when Myrhaug grew up, the drum has been part of his work as a shaman from the very start. He joyfully remembers his first drum journey at a course organized by Ailo Gaup in 1988. Myrhaug's semi-autobiographical book *Sjaman for livet* (*Shaman for Life*, 2011), accentuates the drum as the main instrument in the Saami creation story. He roots his shamanic practice in the traditions connected to the medicine wheel; in Myrhaug's account of creation it is the Saami gods that, by beating their drums, are the originators of this way of structuring the world.

In 1994, Myrhaug bought his first shaman drum, developed by the Saami drum maker Birger Mikkelsen. It was shaped as a frame drum, *gievrie*, but had

Figure 5 The drum that Eirik Myrhaug designed together with shaman Peter Armstrand, which is for sale on his website. Photo: www.livstreet.com/butikk/ samisk-sjamantromme, printed with permission.

no Saami symbols on its membrane. In our conversation Myrhaug related how, at this point, the Saami symbols were still considered taboo, and he decided to avoid decorating the drum in order not to trigger reactions, particularly within the Saami community.

It was not until 2017, in a collaboration with the Saami drum maker Peter Armstrand, that Myrhaug decided to take the drum to a new level and to incorporate Saami symbols and a Saami cosmology on the drum membrane (Fig. 5). The Saami symbols draw inspiration from the Saami life guidance cards developed by shaman Astrid Ingebjørg Swart from Deatnu (Tana). These cards, which resemble a Saami version of the well-known tarot cards, are decorated with Saami gods and goddesses, power animals, and nature elements.[25]

In the same way that Ronald Kvernmo's drum has become a map for a possible Saami shamanistic theology, Myrhaug's drums provide an aesthetic structure and frame for a contemporary interpretation of shamanism. They communicate the most central gods, goddesses, power animals, and symbols,

---

[25] Swart's Saami guideline cards are available at https://www.sarahkkas.com/sarahkkas-veiviserkort.

their position, their relation to each other, and their interactions. The shaman theology conveyed through the drum has a translocal or glocal (Robertson 1995) character. This is a form of shamanism without roots in a particular local context but where Saami symbols, gods, and spiritual powers come together and form new coalitions and fusions. The fact that the role and functions of gods and religious symbols has changed is not new; in order to stay alive and relevant, gods have always adapted to changing environments. What is new in relation to Myrhaug's Saami drum is the context for its usage.

Between 2017 and 2023, shamanism has continued to expand to new arenas, and Myrhaug has been a central catalyst in this expansion. Contemporary eco-crises affect society on all levels, and they have changed how shamanism is articulated and how the drums are applied. The Arctic Shaman Circle was cofounded in November 2018 by forty-five individuals from the entire circum-polar area, with Myrhaug as leader of the board. One of the association's subgoals is to "Contribute and carry out spiritual activism: Actions to support and develop Indigenous peoples' spiritual connection to nature."[26] Shamanism has from the start been a countercultural phenomenon, but within a Nordic context it was not until recently that shamans and drums became directly involved in forms of environmental activism. The overall expressions of this activism include outrage over climate challenges and protest against extractive industries that threaten Indigenous lands and cultures.

In May 2021, a large demonstration, organized by the association Motvind (headwind), took place against the development of wind farms in vulnerable natural areas, particularly against the development of the Øyfjellet wind farm in the Jillen-Njaarke reindeer grazing district. Myrhaug returned as an activist to the Norwegian Parliament building, where forty years earlier he had been the leader of a second hunger strike against the damming of the Alta-Kautokeino river. In 2021, he came as a well-known shaman wearing a *gákti*[27] "armed" with a drum. He held the drum high and started to beat it while discussing the ceremony about to take place, in which he would ask the mountains for assistance in the fight against extractive industries that threaten Indigenous lands. Through the drum, spiritual mountain powers representing the four corners of the world were called upon to take part in the ceremony – Rásttigáisá in the north, Atoklimpen in the east, Hvannadalshnjkur in the west, and Dovrefjell in the south. Drumbeats were heard all over the Parliament square, calling for people's attention. Myrhaug's appeal was short and powerful: "We must stop the sacrifice of nature in our longing for abundance. Extractive industries'

---

[26] See www.arktisksjamansirkel.org/, accessed December 15, 2021.

[27] *Gákti* is the North Saami term for the traditional Saami costume. The *gákti* varies in different Saami areas and language groups.

attack on the reindeer husbandry is a fundamental attack on the Sami way of life. Reindeer husbandry is a carrier and protector of livelihood and culture, also of our spiritual culture."[28] In contrast to the widespread notion of nature as a resource, Myrhaug's appeal was based in his shamanic worldview, which represents a fundamentally new institutional arrangement in which nature is seen as an actor or kin that calls for a radically new relationship between humans and nature.

The 2021 protest reached a wide audience and was featured on many of the national media channels, which led to Myrhaug being invited to events, conferences, and demonstrations throughout the following summer and autumn. For example, he brought his drum to a dialogue meeting with Professor of Biology Dag O. Hessen in order to drum and discuss the ways in which Saami perspectives and spirituality should be activated in the public debate on the management and conservation of nature.[29] On October 11, 2021, the Shamanistic Association announced on Facebook that their own efforts along with those of others had brought about concrete results: the Norwegian Supreme Court had ruled that wind power development at Fosen was illegal. The court stated that it violated the enshrined rights of Indigenous peoples, the Saami, and that all new developments in reindeer husbandry areas should be reviewed. For Myrhaug, along with all of the opponents of wind power development that threatened Indigenous lands, this was an important victory. Myrhaug's example shows how the language of religion and religious symbols can be the means of empowerment vis-à-vis national politics and extractive industries. It also demonstrates that the role of the drums is constantly changing.

Conclusion

Michael Harner was an important catalyst who paved the way for new religious ideas to affect prevailing local practices. This facilitated a revival of the drum as a tool in religious practices. Upon the completion of his training in California, the first Saami shaman, Ailo Gaup, returned with a backpack full of ideas and inspiration about core shamanism, drums, and drum journeys inspired by Harner's teaching. Through Harner, the drum emerged as the primary tool in shamanic practices, as a symbol of continuity with the past. In a contemporary Nordic shamanic context, Saami shamans encounter the drum as a roadmap for a Saami shamanic theology as well as a powerful transformative device.

---

[28] www.facebook.com/per.oestmoen/videos/10225050935924135/, accessed April 15, 2022.
[29] https://x.facebook.com/events/426888455695111?active_tab=discussion, accessed December 15, 2021.

The way the drums have developed into a core element within shamanism in the Nordic countries – as an instrument for soul journeys, for divination, for theology, and as a symbol – reveals that religion-making incorporates complex dynamics of agency (Dressler & Mandair 2011: 22). In Eirik Myrhaug and Ronald Kvernmo's practices and performances, the drum is no longer stigmatized as a reminder of a pagan past but has rather become a powerful, authentic, and magical symbol for a living shamanistic culture. Cultural forms will always be shaped and reshaped. Tradition is not an objective entity with roots in the past and is instead something dynamic and shifting – a contemporary human-made process that facilitates a symbolic construction of relationships between past and present – between roots and routes. The use of drums indicates a complex and multifaceted shamanistic theology emerging, one with a translocal character in which environmentalism and protection of the land are important components. Within Nordic shamanism, the drum has become as an "agent of the sacred" (Gaup 2005: 41) that has the power to open connections for a sustainable future.

2 Contemporary Deposits at Sieidi Offering Places

In November 2016, I (Tiina Äikäs) visited the offering boulder of Taatsi, in Kittilä, Northern Finland, as a part of my fieldwork. What caught my eye, in addition to the stunning landscape, were the various objects that had been left at the site. There were coins, pendants, other personal objects, and modified natural objects, such as a carved stick and a doll made of branches, resting on the platforms and cracks of the stone boulder. Based on my prior knowledge, these kinds of objects are often related to contemporary pagan practices.

I had been to Taatsi a couple of times before and conducted small-scale archaeological excavations there in 2008 (Äikäs 2015: 286–7), but during this visit the growth in the number of contemporary offerings was evident. The *sieidi* of Taatsi – *sieidi* (pl. *sieiddit*) referring to a Saami offering place in North Saami – stands on a deep and rocky shore of the narrow lake Rotkojärvi, which is located about 500 miles upstream from the northwestern end of Lake Taatsinjärvi. The offering place is a natural, high rock column that tapers upwards in a notched manner (Fig. 6). To reach either of its sides, one must climb down the cliff; Parks and Wildlife Finland had torn down the steps that previously led to the shore in the early 2010s, as these had deteriorated and were deemed dangerous (Äikäs & Ahola 2020). The difficulty of the approach has not hindered people from visiting the place, as is demonstrated by the existence of several contemporary deposits in the holes and flat areas of the boulder. There were some deposits already in 2007 when I first surveyed the site, but in the

Figure 6 The sieidi of Taatsi. Photo by Anssi Malinen, used by permission.

following nine years their number had grown, and the variety of different objects had increased.[30]

Material Encounters with the Sieiddit

The contemporary finds at Taatsi could be roughly divided into two groups. The first group consisted of small objects that people often carry with them, most often coins but also pieces of jewelry, buttons, and a token for a shopping trolley. The second group included natural objects such as reindeer bones and antlers, hair, and stones, but also things modified by humans. Someone had left a human figure made of branches and pieces of birch bark that were tied together (Figs. 7 and 8). These items are similar to the contemporary offerings that I have encountered at other sites in Finland and Norway. The reasons for contemporary

---

[30] Interestingly, Kjell Olsen (2017: 235) noted a similar increase in contemporary deposits at the Áhkku sieidi in Norway in the 2010s.

Figure 7 A human figure made of branches documented in 2016.
Photo by Tiina Äikäs, used by permission.

Figure 8 Additional contemporary deposits left at the site in the 2010s.
Photo by Tiina Äikäs, used by permission.

visits can vary from tourism and school visits to more personal connections (e.g., Olsen 2017; Spangen & Äikäs 2020), but here our main interest is in the relations that contemporary pagans and especially shamans have with these places.

Contemporary deposits demonstrate a continuation of animal offerings as well as offerings with no direct link to previous tradition (Äikäs 2015; Äikäs & Spangen 2016; Äikäs et al. 2018). The cache of reindeer antlers, as well as elk skulls seen at one site, appears in accord with the old traditions of offering first game animals and then, from the start of reindeer herding, reindeer meat and antlers. Fish has also been seen among the early offerings (Salmi et al. 2018; Heino et al. 2020; Salmi et al. 2020). The continuation of this practice is evident in the offered fishing gear, such as artificial flies and rods. These contemporary offerings seem to connect with the tradition of giving part of the catch to the sieidi in return for a hunting success that was negotiated with the sieidi before the hunting trips (e.g., Paulaharju 1932; Itkonen 1948a). Sieidi was seen as a living entity with whom people had a reciprocal relationship (cf. Schanche 2004: 1–4). Sieidi could communicate, for example, by moving itself or singing if a time was good for hunting; in return it was given game, fish, or reindeer (e.g., Itkonen 1948b: 308). The sieidi of Taatsi answered the petitioners with a sound like jingling bells coming out of the stone (Paulaharju 1922: 161). However, if a sieidi did not keep its promises, it could be destroyed or abandoned, and, similarly, a sieidi could avenge broken promises (e.g., Holmberg 1915: 31, 35–6; Paulaharju 1932: 26). Today, some of the visitors at sieiddit might ask for hunting success or give thanks for a good catch.

In addition to animal offerings, coins, food items, and personal objects had their counterparts in the older offering tradition. Both archaeological finds and written sources indicate that coins, jewelry, alcohol, tobacco, and food such as cheese were left at the sieidi sites (e.g., Äimä 1903: 115; Paulaharju 1932: 14; Itkonen 1948b: 312; Manker 1957: 88; Äikäs 2015). When it comes to food offerings, only pieces of bottle glass have remained in archaeological material (Äikäs 2015: 201). Some easy-to-carry offerings, such as coins or trolley tokens, could have been left by people with no prior knowledge about offering traditions, who might simply mimic the behavior of previous visitors that they observed from the material remains at the site. Archaeologist Ceri Houlbrook (2018) noted similar behavior while studying the coin trees in Britain, where people press coins into the surface of a tree, hence creating a contemporary tradition. At Áhkku, Seidekjerringa, in Norway, there are several examples of these kinds of pocket holdings, such as small toys, reflectors, and trinkets. This place is known to be visited by tourists and groups from the local school, which would explain more spontaneous behavior rather than a planned offering ritual

(Spangen & Äikäs 2020). In these cases, where frequent visits to the site lead to an accumulation of deposits, the sieidi and the materiality around it affect people's behavior. The existence of offerings encourages more offerings.

Of most interest here are the deposits that show similarities to offerings left at sacred places in different parts of the world by contemporary pagans and other groups inspired by old traditions (Wallis 2003: 171; Blain & Wallis 2007: 10, 56). Natural objects and food items especially fall into this category. There is a general understanding among contemporary pagans that only decomposing material that returns to nature should be left at sacred places, although inorganic materials are often used (e.g., Jonuks & Äikäs 2019). There are numerous examples of offerings similar to other places used by contemporary Pagans. In Taatsi these include, for example, the branch doll, a wooden pendant with a rune symbol and hair tied to it, and pieces of quartzite, as well as quartzite and a small flower bouquet from Kirkkopahta, Muonio. The shared element is the use of natural materials, but one should take note that not all offerings by contemporary pagans are restricted to decomposable materials, as my fieldwork at natural sacred places in Estonia has demonstrated. There the offerings took various forms, many of which will remain permanently at the site if not removed (Jonuks & Äikäs 2019).

To scrutinize the rituals and material relations that contemporary pagans have with sacred places, I conducted a web survey, described in the introduction of this Element. Fifteen of the participants stated that they relate to shamanism, and all of these fifteen reported that they visited sieiddit. Including the responses of all people answering the survey, only 26 percent visited sieiddit. This corresponds to what I learned from an interview conducted earlier for my doctoral dissertation, where a member of a pagan organization said that people visit sieiddit only rarely due to a respect for these places as a part of Saami culture and because they are located far away from big cities (Äikäs 2015: 166). In addition to sieiddit, the respondents identifying themselves in relation to shamanism visited other sacred places in nature, such as cup-marked stones,[31] fells, mountains, springs, and lakes. Thus, not all offerings and offering traditions described in this survey are related to sieiddit.

The material relation with sacred places was strongly evident in survey responses. All respondents mentioned that they leave something at a sacred place. Food was mentioned most often (87 percent), followed by coins (40 percent), drink (13 percent), silver (13 percent), candles (13 percent), and jewelry/pendants (7 percent). Of these, food and drink are hard to trace at sites if they

---

[31] A stone or a cliff on which cup-like hollows were made in the Iron Age, probably in relation to an offering tradition (Kuppikivi, n.d.; Wessman 2010: 89).

have been eaten by animals or absorbed by the soil, but I have encountered candy and snack wrappings and drink bottles – mostly alcohol – from sieiddit. Coins are the most often-found contemporary deposit at sieiddit, but candles or tea lights as well as jewelry and pendants have been found as well. Silver is hard to notice if it has been scratched from a silver bar, as I witnessed at a sacred pond in Southern Finland, but I have found silver pendants, bracelets, and rings from sieiddit. Silver offerings are also mentioned in written sources in relation to old offering traditions (e.g., Paulaharju 1932: 31).

Even though not all of the examples I have noted were decomposing, the emphasis on natural material or even immaterial offerings was more evident when people answered an open question regarding what else they might leave at a sacred place. Of the survey respondents, 60 percent reported that they also left something else apart from the items already mentioned. These objects included reciting a self-made poem or prayer, incense, decomposing handicrafts, decomposing binding, personal hair, herbs, sacred ash, stones, flowers, seeds, cones, straw, bones, and tobacco. People also described their offerings in a more general way as something organic or something beautiful from nature. One response was specifically tied to a certain action – the "first three berries while berry picking." A recurring theme was that only organic or decomposing materials were left at these places, especially something that birds and animals could eat. As one of the respondents stated: "I only want to leave things that do not harm nature but I show my respect and appreciation. All the things that I leave are self-made (having more sentimental value)." In an earlier interview, the interviewee stated that their offerings mainly consist of food, which is left near the sieidi to be consumed by animals and, in this way, return to the circle of nature (Äikäs 2015: 166). These offering practices have a strong connection with the shamanistic milieu's relations to nature, which was emphasized, for example, at the rituals in Isogaisa. Respondents also described their rituals at natural sacred places as being closely tied to their relation to nature, while all of them viewed their connection to nature as important for their spirituality. They saw themselves as part of nature, as described by one of the respondents: "Nature is the source of wisdom and sacredness." Another of the respondents described offering practices as "a strengthening of nature relation through gifts, singing, and prayer. Settling down at sacredness. Finding one's inner peace and strengthening it."

It is nevertheless important to remember that not all offerings were given at sacred places. While visiting the Isogaisa festival in 2014, we also interviewed people about their relation to the offering tradition. There, people described rituals connected to daily life, for example giving a drop of coffee or some food while preparing it. At the festival, people also made offerings by placing them in the fire that burned in the central *lávvu*. These offerings could be food, but one festivalgoer cut pieces of her hair (Äikäs et al. 2018: 6). Offerings that are part of daily activities at home or during a festival can be more spontaneous than the those left at sieiddit.

Embodied Experiences at Sacred Places

Although 80 percent of the respondents mentioned giving offerings, this was not the only activity that took place at the sacred places. Other frequently noted activities that occurred at sacred places were silence (73 percent); touching the sacred object (73 percent); drumming or other music made by oneself or someone else (67 percent); lighting a candle or a fire (67 percent); and singing (53 percent). There were also material aspects in these activities, including "ceremonial equipment," drums, and offerings.

While attending the Isogaisa gathering in 2014 and 2016, we witnessed a ceremony in connection to sieidi offerings as we took part in the excursion to Rikkagallo. We were led there by shaman Eirik Myrhaug, who has organized trips to the sieidi during the Isogaisa festival for several years. During each of the trips, around thirty festival participants with multiple backgrounds were introduced to the walk by Myrhaug and were told how to behave approaching the sieidi. Myrhaug points out that the ancient Saami sites have been in continuous use over the centuries. Although the context and meaning that people have bestowed upon their activities at the sites might have changed, Myrhaug asserts that the continuity of its use boosts the energy and power of the site. He also told the participants to use the two-hour walk to prepare for the encounter with the sieidi, and to think about what they wanted to leave behind, with regard to an item of offering as well as a concern that had brought them on this journey.

After our walk, the 10-meter-high and 12-meter-broad sieidi appeared in front of us, resting in an open valley surrounded by towering mountains. After a short rest, a customary ceremony takes place, one that is used as an introduction to almost all shamanic happenings. Myrhaug calls upon the energies from the four directions, as well as of heaven, Mother Earth, and the universe. Then, each individual participant starts his or her journey towards the stone, walks around it, and places the gift they have brought into the face of the stone.

During the offerings and other rituals, the physicality of the sieidi and that of the visiting person meet. The shape and surface of the sieidi have an effect on how the offerings are placed. At Sieiddakeädgi, in Ochejohka (Utsjoki), several coins have been deposited inside the small hollows in the hole on the side of the sieidi. Samuli Paulaharju (1932: 31), a collector of folklore, has described this

Figure 9 Coins deposited at the cracks of the sieidi stone in Näkkälä.
Photo by Tiina Äikäs, used by permission.

hole as being so deep that a man can almost fit in it, and indeed the placement of offerings here demands some crawling. At Näkkälä, Eanodat (Enontekiö), people have used the cracks on the surface of the stone when placing coins so that they form lines (Fig. 9). In Norway, at Fállegiedgi, Falkesteinen, and Rikkagallo, the split in a cracked stone by the sieidi has been filled with gifts, including antlers, bones, bottles, and fishing gear, demonstrating people interacting with the sieidi through their offerings. (See Spangen & Äikäs 2020.) As the sieidi affects the placement of the offerings, the offerings also have an effect on the sieidi; they change not only how it looks but also its smell and coloring. Historical sources report that sieiddit were smeared with blood and fat (e.g., Paulaharju 1932: 19; Itkonen 1948b: 311), even though there is no direct archaeological evidence of this tradition (cf. Äikäs et al. 2012). The elk skulls left at the sieidi in Kirkkopahta, Muonio, add to the smellscape of the site. They also bring forth new interaction with the sieidi as flies arrive for their feast.

Materiality of the Sacred Landscape

Returning to the sieidi at Taatsi, we note that the materiality of not only the stone but also the surrounding landscape affects the offerings. The site on the shore of Rotkojärvi consists of the boulder called the sieidi of Taatsi as well as a deep cliff with the name of Taatsinkirkko (meaning "a church of Taatsi"), about 100 meters west of the sieidi. Taatsinkirkko is also known to be a sacred place for the Saami (Paulaharju 1932: 50). During excavations in 2008, it became evident that most of the old offerings found were from the area between the sieidi and Taatsinkirkko. I have argued elsewhere that the placement of offerings in this area might have been due to the belief that this was the location of interaction between the sacred places (Äikäs 2012: 87). The sieiddit were considered to be living entities, and in the case of Taatsi this idea was reinforced by its shape, which resembled a human figure, and the jingling voice that was heard from the stone (Paulaharju 1922: 161). There was also a notable echo at Taatsinkirkko (Paulaharju 1932: 5), and this effect, produced by the deep cliffs at the site, is still part of the experience at Taatsi (Rainio et al. 2018). This might well have created the experience of a communicating sieidi.

In the beginning, the contemporary offerings were also placed at the western side of the sieidi stone. Whether this was due to the line of sight to Taatsinkirkko or to the fact that this side was easier to reach from the wooden steps and platform is uncertain. After the removal of the steps and platform in the 2010s, the majority of the offerings have been left on the eastern side of the stone, which is now easier to approach using a narrow path on the steep hill as opposed to the rockier western side. The actions of Parks and Wildlife Finland in the maintenance of the site have therefore influenced the way people act on it.

Another example where Parks and Wildlife Finland and the local tourist entrepreneur, Visit Inari, have shaped the materiality of the sacred place and the embodied experiences of the visitors comes from Ukonsaari Island (Äijihsuálui) in Anár (InariSa Aanaar, Inari). In 2019, an opinion piece in the national newspaper *Helsingin Sanomat* by the Inari Saami Inka Musta and archaeologist Eeva-Kristiina Harlin opened a discussion on whether people should be allowed to land on this sacred island (Harlin & Musta 2019). A comparison was drawn to the Uluru in Australia, where climbing on the Aboriginal sacred place is discouraged. The discussion led to two results: Visit Inari decided to stop landing on the island and now has its ship circumnavigate the island; and Parks and Wildlife Finland tore down the platforms and steps on the island. Now visitors can view the well-known and magnificent profile of the island, but any direct physical interaction is discouraged.

Tourism operators frequently play a large role in the kind of bodily experiences that visitors gain at the sites. In some cases, a prepared performance is planned to give visitors a multisensoral embodied experience in which tourism and shamanism mingle. While writing my doctoral dissertation in 2011, I conducted an email interview with the Shaman of Nulituinen, Veikko Siitonen, an entrepreneur who at that time took tourists to the sieidi of Taatsi for shamanistic performances. Siitonen stated that approximately forty to sixty persons between the ages of ten and seventy from all around the world attend these performances. According to Siitonen, the meetings include eating, prayers, silence, conversations, and healing, since people's motivation for attending the meetings comes from a desire to gain closeness to nature or Indigenous religion. According to his website, a visit to the sieidi is also part of a drum making course, during which the drums are blessed at the sieidi (Siitonen 2019).

Creation of Sieiddit

Even though some of the practices related to sieiddit are relatively new and their connection to old beliefs varies, in some cases the historicity of the tradition and the sieidi are emphasized. This is the case at Rikkagallo, where a sign in front of the sieidi refers to a source that describes the its historical position within the Saami community.

The antiquity of the tradition is highlighted in both the ritual and the Isogaisa festival itself. During religious rituals and festivals, pagans, as Harvey argues, "regularly renew their relationships and deepen their intimacy with their environment" (Harvey 2009: 8). The ritual at Rikkagallo can be linked to Madeline Duntley's observations about contemporary religious practitioners' relations and use of the Mount Shasta pilgrimage site in California. She writes: "To spiritual tourists this mountain offers its most renewable resource, a 'universal supply' of wisdom that is oriented towards the future, but anchored to the past" (Duntley 2015: 144). The sieidi Rikkagallo revises the way the past appears by opening up a Saami history and landscape. In the ritual, the sieidi comes to represent connections and continuities with the past, but at the same time, new meanings are added and new connections are made through the approaches of individual participants, their offerings, and their visions of the future.

Tourist experiences can also take place at sites, where authenticity lies more in stories than in physical places. As Richard Prentice (2001: 15–22) has stated, the experience of authenticity does not demand historicity of a place but can also be constructed by recreating the atmosphere of the original place and by conveying emotions and experiences that can be credibly related to it. This was evident at Kalliorova in Muonio, Finland, where I encountered a local tourist entrepreneur who told me that he had been taking tourists to a stone that "looked like a sieidi" and that a "shaman" comes to meet the tourists and performs a "Lappish baptism"[32] (Äikäs 2015: 169.) This tourist practice has been sternly criticized as it depicts a picture of magical Lapland and exoticizes Saaminess using modified Saami elements such as fake Saami gákti (Ruotsala

---

[32] A tourist experience where a person dressed as a shaman tells creation stories and at the end initiates people as a part of Lapland or the magic of Lapland.

2008: 52; Flemmen & Kramvig 2016; Kramvig & Flemmen 2018; Mathisen 2020*)*. This image was so popular that it was still used in 2015 by VisitFinland, which promotes tourism in Finland. The organization received criticism from the Non-Discrimination Ombudsman for promoting a stereotypical and misleading picture of Saami culture (Lakkala 2015). I have elsewhere (Äikäs 2015) criticized the idea of identifying sieiddit based on their appearance, since sieiddit can be of various shapes and sizes, and in some cases, they do not differ from the rest of the stones around them. But the idea of a typical appearance of a sieidi remains strong. In the case of Kalliorova, what was seen as sieidi-like was the pyramid-like form of the stone, whereas in actuality the sieidi located on the hill in question has been described not as pyramid-like but as lying on four stones (Pääkkönen 1902: 19), and its location is not confirmed.

On the shore of Äkässaivo, also in Muonio, Parks and Wildlife Finland has raised signs informing visitors of the history of the site. Historical sources describe offering cliffs that surround the sacred *sáiva* lake (Paulaharju 1922: 198). The sign indicating an offering cliff is nevertheless further away from the shore, by a prominent but not historically confirmed rock formation. The archaeological excavations by this rock revealed no ancient offerings but instead a small number of contemporary deposits consisting of snuff, a piece of cold smoked reindeer meat, and a Christian tract. These seem to indicate that the sign raised at the place has created not only an offering tradition but also a Christianization of the place (Äikäs 2015: 193).

Tourism and contemporary deposits can therefore create new places in the vicinity of old offering places but also in new locations. The interviews conducted at Isogaisa showed that an old tradition connected to the sieidi was not always requisite for a ritual connection. People had respect for the old sites and their link to past generations and could even feel a special energy at these sites, but they had their own personal sieiddit. One of the interviewees stated that a stone chooses you (Äikäs et al. 2018: 10). Another interviewee at Isogaisa claimed that he has his own sieiddit, just as his ancestors had their own ones. Here the tradition of having your own places was more important than visiting the old sieidi places. As one interviewee puts it: "In my belief, you make your own sacred places. Because when my ancestors were shamans and they had a sacred place, they built it themselves. And I have my sacred place, on my place. ... I don't think it's necessary to go to the old ones when you can make your own" (Äikäs et al. 2018: 10–11).

The personal connection with the place was also evident from the responses from the web survey, where 73 percent of the respondents stated that their own experience at the site informed them of the sacredness of the place. Somewhat paradoxically, however, 87 percent said that they visit sites that are known to the wider public. Of course, this does not exclude personal experiences of sacredness but does show that personal experience can be an added value at sites of which knowledge was also gained from oral tradition, Internet sources, academic publications, and maps, since people could choose several options while answering this question. There were also those sacred places that were not publicly known. With a possibility of choosing several options, 53 percent of the respondents stated that they visit sites that are known only to them or sites that only people close to them know (60 percent).

A Place or a Material Relation?

It seems that a multifaceted interplay between historicity, materiality, and the agency of a place is occurring at the sieiddit. Kjell Olsen (2017) has stated that sieiddit are "contested spaces where different actors aim to impose their own categorizations of how sieiddit are to be understood" but that they seem to have an agency of their own. Shamanism and shamans regulate sieiddit by creating "proper" ways to interact with the sieiddit. For example, the rule of not leaving inorganic materials at the sacred place is confirmed by 73 percent of our respondents who follow shamanism, and 86 percent of all respondents. At the same time, sieiddit have their own agency and contribute to regulating shamanism through their form, connection to landscape, and history. Experiences are shaped by the contact between human beings, the sieiddit, the landscape, and the offerings. As folklorist Anne Eriksen points out, the role of monuments, such as Rikkagallo, Taatsi, and other sieiddit, is to contribute to a dialogue between memory and history. At the same time, these monuments have a double function in the context of memory, in reminding us of bygone history as well as reminding participants of the value the place possessed in the past and still possesses. "Through their materiality and accessibility, they also serve as *connection hubs*. This is where history and the individual meet, and something happens: A personal experience; fertile ground for one's own memories" (Eriksen 1999: 95, italics in original).

But the historicity of the sieidi or any other sacred place is a complex phenomenon. When asked if it is important that the place was used as a sacred place in history, 54 percent of the respondents said yes, 33 percent somewhat, and for 13 percent, it was not important. One respondent commented: "It is nice to feel a connection to the past generations at known sacred places, but it is not necessary for experiencing sacredness." The connection to the past could also be questioned: "I feel that I am (at least seemingly) part of a continuation and revitalizing (again at least seemingly) something that has been before."

Several respondents also mentioned the energy or the "väki"[33] of the sacred places. "Certain places have exceptionally strong 'väki' or force and those are the places to which people have returned through centuries and millennia." So, people come because of the energy, and at the same time there is energy because people have come for a long time.

But, as noted, historicity can also be gained from traditions apart from specific places. People continued a tradition in a place that they chose themselves or that had chosen them. It therefore seems that the material relation to a place can be more important than the historicity of the place. The sacredness is not always tied to old places but rather new relations to sites through material relations and history-making. The offering rituals, with their connection to past practices as well as to ritual creativity, also connect the new sacred places to the perceived historicity of shamanism.

3 Power Animals: Embodied Practices in Shamanism and Popular Culture

This Section (By Tiina Äikäs) focuses on power animals, which have been central to shamanism from the earliest teachings of Michael Harner. With shamanism's spread to new arenas, the power animal category has become adapted to local traditions, cultures, and climates. The spread of power animals to regional climates offers a window into exchanges between global and local shamanic currents. It also reveals how the reclaiming of space-specific traditions is expressed in material dynamics that extend the relationship between the secular and the sacred.

Power Animals' Position among Shamans in Norway and Finland

Harner introduced the concept of power animals in *The Way of the Shaman* (1980: 57–72), and their popularity quickly spread to the wider New Age scene. A number of books within the New Age category, published beginning in the 1990s, thematize the spiritual properties of animals (see Kraft 2000). Initially, dolphins and whales were designated as the most spiritually wise beings, but gradually other animals have been included in the category of power animals.

This broad approach makes it easy to adapt the power animal category to almost any culture. Contemporary power animals, and the rituals in which contact and relations with a personal power animal are established, have become central to all shamanic organizations and groups within Norway and Finland. The power animals of Harner's core shamanism are linked to notions of collective animal souls rather than to individual animals. Finnish shaman Johannes Setälä describes power animals as entities that are often connected to personal inner growth and

---

[33] An impersonal supernatural force inhabiting places or objects in Finnish folk belief (Stark 2002: 47).

act as guides on spiritual journeys – especially on difficult ones (Setälä 1997: 75; Setälä 2005: 50; cf. Boekhoven 2013: 245). The website of Lehto ry (the Association for the Animistic Religions in Finland) states that spirit helpers (usually power animals) help on spirit journeys, or with identifying causes of illnesses, and with bringing back lost souls (Lehto – Shamanismi, n.d.). The idea that power animals do not solely appear to shamans but can be accessed by everyone is also common. The Shaman Association (Fi) declares that "each person has their own power animal, guardian spirit, or angel" (Kouri 2022). Hence, power animals have a dual meaning as beings connected to the work of shamans as well as beings that are accessible for everyone.

Setälä states that power animals are not static. His own animal helper changed its form from a wolf to a hawk so that it could travel long journeys quickly (Setälä 2005: 51). The concept of a spirit helper seems to be a more general term that also includes power animals. The website of the Shaman Association (Fi) notes that the term power animal in shamanism is typically used since spirits often manifest in an animal form. Spirits or forces choose the form that is most suitable for the person in question. The same spirit can have several manifestations. Thus, spirit helpers are not limited to a single sphere but can be found in the Underworld while seeking strength or to cure an illness and in the Upper World when a person is in need of guidance or teaching (Kouri 2022).

In Norway, power animals became central to the practice of shamanism from the movement's nascent spread in the mid-1980s. Ailo Gaup elaborates on the meaning of power animals in *The Shamanic Zone*, where he points out that power animals have the ability to teach us about nature and bridge the contemporary human–nature divide (2005: 46). In the shamanic environment in both Finland and Norway, the concept of nature has come to represent opposition to globalization, technology, and modernization. Similarly, nature has been featured as a symbol of truth and personal growth. It represents an overall symbol of all that is good, original, and stimulating. Power animals can be seen as manifestations of these notions of nature's properties and the power of nature. Gaup argues that the materiality of a recording can be used as a substitute if one cannot access the sounds of live nature. The materiality of a recording has a democratizing effect that makes Nordic fauna and its animal sounds accessible to shamanic seekers on a global scale.

Embodied Power Animals

Embodied practices and experiences are promoted as important elements in rituals and for the production of sacred space (Holloway 2003: 1964). Many religious or spiritual practices often include bodily engagement, and there is a relationship between the material body and spiritual qualities or forces

(Fowler 2011). Embodied experiences such as seeing, touching, hearing, and feeling are intertwined with ephemeral experiences such as dreams, imagination, and visions (Morgan 2012). There is also a connection between materiality and embodiment (Crossland 2012) when people use objects in their embodied practices and bodily engage with materialities.

Embodied elements of shamanism were strongly present at Isogaisa, with meetings around the central fire, a festival hugger (a volunteer who has been tasked with giving hugs to festival participants), drumming, and yoiking. A festival dance has also been part of the festival since 2011. In the dance, the Saami musician Elin Kåven mimics the movements of animals, thereby bringing the idea of animals into the perceptions and movements of festival attendees. The dance can be experienced during the festival or via YouTube, where it was online prior to the festival in 2011, and people are encouraged to learn the steps before arriving at the festival (Kaaven 2011). While performing at Isogaisa, Kåven wears skins and a pair of reindeer antlers. Her dance mimics the movements and sounds of various Arctic animals, including the sparrow, the bear, the reindeer, and the eagle, as well as natural elements such as the sun and water. The central role of animals was also evident when Kåven performed in the Eurovision Song Contest final in 2017 in a duo, "Elin & The Woods." In this performance, yoik (luothi), a Saami shaman drum and three "spirit animals" – a polar fox, a wolf, and a reindeer – were central elements (Kalvig 2020). As Kalvig notes, "Sami people as producers, and Sami religion and spirituality as semiotic resources, offer all of us to join in the ritualization of these resources through popular culture. The material enables the experience of the Sami as a living version of animism, where we are 'As One'" (Kalvig 2020: 170).

Johannes Setälä (1997: 25) states that a dance to a power animal, as well as shamanistic singing and drumming or playing another instrument, is an essential part of a shamanistic session. The Second Shamanic Gathering and Conference in Finland in summer 2022 included "a dance of the five animals" by Johanna Hurme (Shamaaniseura ry 2022a). Here dance is used as a way of healing: "we will find the spirits of these animals within us and create our own unique dance with them. We will ask for help from these animals' spirits to guide us forward in our healing path." Hurme states that she uses embodiment and dance as a way to explore the connection to nature (Shamaaniseura ry 2022a).

Embodied practices can also be a way to keep contact with one's power animal. One of our interviewees points out that she had asked the eagle how to stay in contact; in response, a tendon yarn[34] dropped on her head. She

---

[34] A yarn made of the vessels of reindeer and used for sewing leather clothes. Tendon was pulled from the reindeer's back skin or more rarely leg and then dried. See "Lanka, jännelanka," www .finna.fi/Record/museovirasto.BF34AE903DD58C636CF5F13A21A505ED.

interpreted this as a sign that she can maintain contact by making handicrafts. According to her, not all connections need to be material, but handicraft can be one way to keep contact with both the Spirit World and the people for whom one creates the items. Handicraft is emotional work where one is connected to one's emotions and to observing them. Emotions come through your body to your fingertips when you work on the material.[35] Here keeping in contact with one's power animal is intertwined with embodied practices of making handicraft and with establishing emotional bonds with other people.

Materiality of Power Animals

As the case of handicraft demonstrated, materiality and embodiment are intertwined. The costume that Kåven wears while performing the Isogaisa dance brings the materiality of shamanism to her skin. Wearing clothing, therefore, can be an important embodied activity and marker of identity as it can be used as a way to express one's personality (e.g., Horn & Gurel 1981). Archaeologist Chris Fowler (2010: 360) has emphasized the connection between identity and material culture. "The practices by which people make things, live with them, and use them also make those people, so the process of objectification is also a process of personification. Identities are produced out of the ongoing interactions between people and things" (Fowler 2010: 366). For example, garments can be used to convey ethnic or religious identity.

At the market in Isogaisa, one can buy clothes with animal symbols (Fig. 10 and 11). One of the vendors is the shaman Lone Beate Ebeltoft, whose design firm, Alveskogen, specializes in clothes and accessories inspired by the Middle Ages and Arctic Indigenous clothing. Wolves, bears, eagles, and reindeer are especially in evidence, representing the animal world. In addition, Ebeltoft uses symbols from Saami drums and from prehistoric rock art. At Isogaisa, clothing not only represents people but also constitutes who they are (Äikäs & Fonneland 2021). The clothes and designs by Ebeltoft are an example of the material engagement in the production of Saami shamanism (see also Kalvig 2020), with symbols from the past being reclaimed and reused in the present to form shamanistic identities (Äikäs & Fonneland 2021).

Even though wearing a cape with a wolf or bear depicted on it seems like a clear demonstration of a connection to a certain animal, power animals can be portrayed in various garments, not all of which are related to shamanism or even to spirituality. Artist Joni Aikio, who specializes in paintings of power animals, asserts that people usually have some kind of connection to the animals whose picture they want to hang on their wall. This connection is not necessarily related to shamanism

---

[35] Anonymous, phone Interview with T. Äikäs, June 1, 2022.

Figure 10 and 11 Luhkka with power animals, designed by Lone Beate Ebeltoft.
Photo: Lone Beate Ebeltoft, used by permission.

or power animals, however. Such images may work as reminders, as things to consider that suggest the characteristics they would like to have. According to Aikio, "if one feels too tamed or too incorporated into the society, a wolf can bring wildness and detachment. Bear is powerful and strong, but it prepares for winter. Certain animals have similar associations for many people."[36] The artist believes that the spectrum of power animals has grown, and that people have turned from mythical animals to a more complex idea of power animals. He states that power animals can balance one's own personality, that is, one can seek in the power animal those aspects one is lacking. But the emphasis nevertheless remains in wild animals, "not often a hen or a cow, or other tamed animals as we already feel that we are tamed in the society." Contrary to the general depiction of reindeer as a northern power animal, Aikio feels that the semidomesticated reindeer might appear too tame to be a power animal.

The symbols of power animals travel from one context to another. For example, Joni Aikio was asked to design a casket cover (Fig. 12) for the company Peaceful, which sells ecological caskets and personal casket covers. Its website states that "the casket cover tells a story about the life and personality of the

Figure 12 A casket cover designed by Joni Aikio depicting power animals in a mountain landscape. This casket cover, produced by Peaceful, was named Voimaeläin (Power Animal). Copyright: Joni Aikio/Peaceful. Photo used by permission.

---

[36] J. Aikio, personal interview with T. Äikäs, January 31, 2022.

deceased" (Peaceful n.d.). The relation of a deceased to Aikio's mountain land-scape with (power) animals may vary from the spiritual to the mundane, but the artist's purpose is to offer a casket cover that is empowering. The animals on this casket cover come from Finnish wildlife, including reindeer, bear, swan, elk, and wolf, according to Aikio.

Power animals are also depicted in jewelry. The firm TaigaKoru (MagicJewelry), for example, does not mention power animals on its website (Taigakoru n.d.), but says that the design of its jewelry is partly based on folk tradition connected to "shaman drums." Shamans are here described as healers and diviners that called spirits to their help by drumming until they reached a trance state, wherein they could turn into animals. The website shows a picture of a drumming shaman, and on the drum are the different symbols that TaigaKoru uses in its jewelry, including the bear, wolf, crane, black-throated diver, salmon, beaver, and reindeer. These items are frequently sold in jewelry stores in Finland and bought for personal use and as gifts.

Power Animals in Secular Arenas

As noted by Chidester, "popular culture operates at the intersection of new technologies of cultural production, new modes of cultural consumption, and new strategies for imagining human possibility. These innovations have made a dramatic difference in the ways in which religion intersects with popular cultural formations" (Chidester 2018: 178). As the examples of casket covers and jewelry show, power animals have moved to arenas other than those related directly to shamanism. In April 2022, a video game called Skábma (Snowfall) was released by Red Stage Entertainment, a small, independent game studio in Finland. In this game, Saami Indigenous spiritual themes are invoked through virtual visits to a sieidi, using a drum, and meeting power animals to "Harness the powers of the Noaidi Drum and the Familiar Spirits to fight against a disorder spreading across the land!" (Steam n.d.). The game description seems to present the traditional Saami spirituality as threatened by the more agrarian lifestyle:

> The daily life of a Sámi village is disturbed after an accident at a nearby Tar-Burning Pit. An odd disease starts spreading across the area, affecting every-thing from the land to the people and animals. You play as Áilu, a young Sámi herder searching for a runaway reindeer doe. The mystery of the growing disorder starts to unravel when Áilu finds an old, enchanted drum, Goavddis. . . . Find the four Familiar Spirits and reconnect with nature to find the source of the disease. It's your time to become a new Noaidi for a new era! Find four familiar spirits, Skuolfi – The Owl, Guovža – The Bear, Čámsa – The Trout and Rieban – The Fox, with varying powers affecting your movement and ability to Attune the Disorder spreading through Sámiland. (Steam n.d.)

Figure 13 Guiding spirits, such as the bear, owl, fox, and horned fish, help the player in the game Skábma. Image from game. (Image with permission from Red Stage Entertainment Oy.)

The game summary highlights the role of noaiddit in saving nature in the belief that the traditional spirituality creating "a new noaidi for a new era" can help to save nature. In the game, "nature is calling for noaiddit" because earth is in danger. The drum is depicted as an object of might, which heals both people and the environment, and a noaidi can harness its powers. There is also a connection between the guiding spirits (*veahkkevuoiŋŋat*) in animal form and the drum, as the former are depicted on the latter (Fig. 13). Skábma also emphasizes the role of arctic animals as spirit helpers as the encountered guiding spirits include an owl, a bear, a horned fish, a fox, and a reindeer.

Skábma is not the only venue through which guiding spirits or power animals have entered popular culture. There seems to be a growing trend to introduce power animals to a general audience as guides to self-knowledge. Even when the link between materiality and spirituality seems evident, as in the case of power animal cards, users might not be familiar with shamanism or identify themselves in relation to it. The cards and associated book, *Pohjolan voimaeläimet* (*Nordic Power Animals*) by Maaretta Tukiainen and Markus Frey (2018), are used in order to identify one's personal traits.

As the artist Aikio asserted, the emphasis is on one's self-knowledge and personal growth, not on a shamanistic search for one's power animal. Tukiainen and Frey's book focuses on teaching Nordic mythology. The trend toward aiming power animal cards and books to a more general audience also becomes clear in light of the rise in power animal workshops for children. One of these was organized in May 2022 at the local library in Lauritsala, Finland. The workshop used Nordic power animal cards as inspiration in an art class, was aimed at children between five and twelve years old.

As Chidester has noted, this "dynamic materiality of religion" has enabled symbols of Indigenous religion to be used in various contexts. According to him:

> Indigenous religion can also be fluid and mobile in transaction with a changing world. At the same time, the diffusion of religious impulses through popular culture, which animate personal subjectivities, can form communities of sacred solidarity, direct desire toward sacred objects, and facilitate relations of sacred exchange that replicate features associated with Indigenous religion. (Chidester 2018: 209)

Skábma is a genuine initiative, scripted by Saami Marjaana Auranen (Eira-Teresá Joret Mariánná) and featuring characters speaking North Saami. The computer game brings Indigenous spirituality with drums, sieiddit, and spirit helpers/power animals into the sphere of popular culture. With its English instructions, it makes Saami mythology accessible in a global way and raises awareness of Saami culture as it has already attracted international attention (Jussila 2022; Last 2022).

Power Animals as Metaphor

All in all, power animals are not only shamanistic helpers but also powerful metaphors that can be used in representing humans' connection to nature, their personality, or history. The link between Saami spirituality and power animals comes from the idea of a people living in close connection to nature and has its roots in the animistic worldview and spirit helpers of the noaiddit. It is not surprising, therefore, that power animals have also been used as a way to teach about Saami culture. For example, the Espoo School of Arts has organized power animal workshops for school children. During the workshop, children are told about the Saami culture and connection to nature while they model their own power animals out of clay. The emphasis is more on teaching about the connection to nature than about Saami religion or spirituality in general. In the workshop, power animals create a link between nature, Saami culture and history, and the children's own activity. The organizers are aware that, as such, power animals were not part of Saami history, but the organizers nevertheless feel that they can be used in order to talk about the close relation that Saami culture had with nature and animals.[37] At the same time, the idea of power animals gives something concrete and tangible that children can create with their own hands as they mold their own power animals from natural clay and then leave them in their chosen place in the woods. The process is supposed to give them an embodied, haptic connection to nature, which materialized the history of Saami in the suburbs of southern Finland.

---

[37] Anonymous, personal interview with T. Äikäs, January 18, 2022.

The computer game Skábma also creates the image of the Saami as an environmentally friendly people. This construction of community and common values is closely intertwined with a production of cultural differences (see Mathisen 2000; Olsen 2000). Where the original emphasis on closeness to nature and the forces of nature was what placed Saami culture at the lowest stages of the evolutionary ladder, today those characteristics locate them at the highest. Anthropologist Jonathan Friedman writes:

> [The] Indigenous is now part of a larger inversion of Western cosmology in which the traditional other, a modern category, is no longer the starting point of a long and positive evolution of civilization, but a voice of Wisdom, a way of life in tune with nature, a culture in harmony, a gemeinschaft, that we have all but lost. (Friedman 1999: 391)

This way of constructing Saami societies as distinctly different can be said to rest on a primitivist tendency, building up stereotypical representations of Saami as a type of "noble savage" and as children of nature. Several researchers have attributed the construction of frozen images that tend to be immutable to this form of framing the Saami (see Carpenter 1973; Kulick & Wilson 1992; Mathisen 2010). Even though these are cultural images that have been produced from the outside, they are also images and myths that representatives from Indigenous cultures themselves have appropriated and are building on. In Skábma, Saami religions are no longer culturally stigmatized, nor are they a reminder of a pagan past, but rather serve as powerful and magical symbols of living Saami culture and an economic and social resource in the negotiation and reinterpretation of local identities.

Folklorist Dell Hathaway Hymes (1975: 345–69) refers to this type of cultural production process as traditionalization. The term describes the processes that take place when selected cultural expressions are inscribed in a discourse on tradition and continuity. Questions of origin are not relevant in this context, since traditions, in light of the traditionalization process, can be portrayed as selective, symbolic constructions of the past in the present. According to folklorists Richard Handler and Jocelyn Linnekin (1984), a distinction between true and false traditions is to a small extent suitable for understanding these types of processes. This is also the prevailing perspective within large parts of cultural research today, where tradition is no longer understood as a static transfer of goods from the past to the present but instead considered to be a simultaneous, selective, and symbolic construction, where certain aspects of the present are linked with selected parts of the past. The value that the power animals convey through Skábma is thus not related to the fact that these elements have an "organic value" that has accompanied them through the ages, but rather that they are assigned value through discourses that have hegemony in contemporary times. These discourses are in turn connected to political, economic, and social relations and intervene in various types of power relations in the present (Mathisen 2000: 19).

In Skábma, the production of cultural values, the dissemination of images of the Saami Indigenous people as a people living in contact with nature and as being a holistic society in close contact with the spiritual world, can be seen as an active, conscious, and strategic use of a symbolic resource. This is how Skábma is more than just a game. It opens up insight into a wide range of political, social, and cultural discourses that are active in Sápmi today. It can be said to provide insight into ethnopolitical processes and cultural negotiations where certain elements are chosen in favor of others and where the end product has the power to influence our image of Saami culture in the present.

Arctic Power Animals

We have seen an emphasis on arctic animals in the selection of power animals for a computer game, songs, cards, and jewelry, as well as clothes. In an interview, Lone Beate Ebeltoft underlines how many people, inspired by Harner and his core shamanism, would choose a large, powerful animal like the bear, the eagle, and the wolf, and, by decorating clothes with these animals, would highlight and claim their "shamanistic identity." But she also states that the use of power animals as decorations has generated criticism as well:

> Some people criticized this type of design. They pointed out that it was unethical to have symbols on clothes, and especially symbols of animals and nature. In the old noaidi tradition, there was a saying that the most powerful noaiddit could bind an animal spirit to themselves and use this spirit as a helper in the spiritual world. Also the noaidi could send his or her free soul into a living animal, a bird, a fish, or an insect, and partly control it to find out things and gain insight. I still do not see many Saami shamans who put animal symbols on their clothes, but an awakening is happening right now. Due to the increasing presentation of Saami symbols in social media, more people request clothes with these kinds of motifs.[38]

Ever since Harner, power animals tend to be those with high symbolic capital in Western culture and mythology, such as bears, foxes, deer, and porpoises, as well as dragons (see Harner 1980). In the Nordic shamanism discussed in this section, these animals have been accompanied by those grounded in arctic fauna, such as the polar bear, the reindeer (and particularly the white reindeer), the polar fox, and the eagle. As we have stated, "the preferred guardian spirits

---

[38] L. B. Ebeltoft, personal interview with T. Äikäs, February 2, 2021.

seem to be wild and physically powerful animals that are related to heroic images of strength, smartness, and wisdom" (Äikäs & Fonneland 2021: 5). Domesticated animals seem to be considered less powerful, with the exception of the semidomesticated reindeer, which has long roots in Saami culture and ritual symbolism (Äikäs 2015; Heino et al. 2020; Salmi & Seitsonen 2022). The material culture related to shamanism – from computer games to power animal cards and clothes – places an emphasis on traditional, arctic animals. The idea of Nordic shamanism seems to influence which animals are seen as proper power animals, since Nordic animals have a central role in the power animal imagery of popular culture. Nevertheless, as our interviews have demonstrated, power animals do not always stem from the local fauna.

Lately, there have also been critics of Harner's emphasis on powerful wild animals. As the shaman Kyrre Franck, from the Shamanistic Association in Norway, argues: "I need to talk to you about spirit animals. You know wolf is getting overworked. And squirrel, well squirrel, he's getting a bit lonely" (Äikäs & Fonneland 2021: 5). Franck is diverting attention from the dominant, powerful wild animals to those that are closer to us.

Conclusion

Power animals are both spiritual – appearing in shamanistic sessions and during meditation – and secular, easy to materialize in clothes, jewelry, and cards. Power animals are strongly linked to embodied practices, as they are approached by drumming, dancing, and doing handicrafts. The website of SA (Fi) expresses this intertwined materiality and embodied practices: "[Shamanism m]ay use instruments, land, elements, voice, dance/movement, art and crafting, story-telling to access and express these realms" (Shamaaniseura ry 2022b).

Power animals also have agency of their own: they can choose to whom they appear, and in which form they manifest themselves. In addition, power animals belong not only to shamans but also to every one of us, a fact that was also emphasized at Isogaisa. This might be one reason why power animals have moved from a strictly shamanistic context to other spiritual practices and into popular culture. They are present in different material forms and in clothing, jewelry, and drums as well as on casket covers. As power animals have moved into popular culture, they have also been presented in games, on social media, and on YouTube. These elements have then again moved back to contemporary shamanism as YouTube is used for sharing the Isogaisa dance and Facebook for creating pages for shamanistic groups.

Power animals are shaped by global trends and political concerns. They are spiritual beings, but they have also become symbols for a sustainable future in a time of environmental concerns and nature crisis. This expansion has served to increase their powers and authority, but also their fluid transition between religion and the secular. Shamanism is not an isolated phenomena but rather interacts with the wider culture industry, of which the move of power animals from spiritual milieus to popular culture is a good example.

4 Chagabusiness: Mushrooming a Shaman Entrepreneurship

This section (by Trude Fonneland) takes as its starting point a mushroom that over the last ten years has become important in several shamanistic environments in Nordic countries – as mythology, medicine, economics, tourism, a producer of sacred space, and a commodity for personal consumption and enjoyment. The fungus in mind is the mushroom known as chaga (Báhkkololmmai in North Saami), or *Inonotus obliquus*.[39] The section concentrates on the development of one particular shaman enterprise in a remote community in northern Norway for which chaga has emerged as significant.[40] I follow the new lives of chaga, the literally mushrooming popularity of this fungus, by focusing on a single entrepreneur, the shaman Ronald Kvernmo. What facilitates a chaga business, and what kind of restrictions and opportunities exist for this particular case of professional shamanship? How does chaga create new imprints, relations, regulations, policies, and possibilities; and, conversely, how is chaga shaped by shamanism?

Background

Chaga is a fungal species that grows parasitically mainly on birch in the northern hemisphere. It has a long history within the field of Saami folk medicine (Steen 1961; Dunfjeld 1998) (Fig. 14). Chaga is easily recognizable due to its tumor-like shape and its hard, dark brown surface and has become an integral part of the shamanic environment in Nordic countries. It has brought about new concepts, rituals, and economies that leave traces within both the shamanistic environments and society in general.

---

[39] In Norwegian, the word for chaga is *kreftkjuke* (cancer mushroom), a word most likely related to the growth's tumor-like shape and looks, and that it has been used as a folk medicine in relation to different cancer diseases. The shamans I have interviewed use the Norwegian name to a lesser extent and prefer chaga, the Russian and English term. Chaga is also the name used in the product's marketing. This is probably related to the fact that the fungus was introduced as chaga to the shamans in an international context, and that using an international term is a better strategy for marketing purposes.

[40] Chaga has become a prominent materiality in Finland as well within contemporary shaman entrepreneurships. On the website ValonTalo (House of Light), which offers shamanistic healing, chaga is marketed as a product that might strengthen the healing process. On a linked blog page, "ValonTalo: Shamanistinen elämäntapa ja parantaminen" (House of Light: Shamanistic Lifestyle and Healing), the author describes using chaga for improving the well-being of the body. The author refers to previous use of chaga in treatment of cancer and tuberculosis but notes that this kind of use has been criticized (ValonTalo 2015).

Figure 14 Chaga powder and chaga drink presented at Kvernmo's website, https://isogaisa.org/chaga-info/ used by permission.

Ceremonial spiritual hallucinogens have an insignificant position in Nordic shamanism. Ayahuasca and peyote are not native to the Nordic region and are also illegal to keep and ingest according to the current penal code.[41] The situation is different with chaga. This is a mushroom known in local folk medicine. It is common in Nordic flora and not considered a hallucinogen and thus is not affected by the penal code. Harvesting chaga in a Norwegian context is also linked to the right of public access (Allemannsretten). Allemannsretten is the basis for outdoor life in Norway and is often used as a collective term for the rights people have to the free use of nature, including harvesting.[42] This law makes chaga a common good and something that everyone can harvest and use at their own discretion.

A Chaga Entrepreneurship Takes Shape

How did the recognition of chaga take place? Stories about chaga started to show up in Norway around 2010 in various shamanic arenas, such as organized drum journeys, alternative fairs, and festivals. The shamanic environment can best be described as a dynamic milieu in which people seek inspiration from a broad range of sources. One development that stood out in the Nordic shamanic environment at that time was the establishment of the Saami shamanic festival Isogaisa (see Fonneland 2015, 2017b, and this Element). From the very start, this festival sought cooperation with Saami communities across Sápmi to establish a bond between Saami cultural works and to promote dialogue around Indigenous histories, cultures, and religions, on Indigenous terms. Yearly institutions, such as the Sámediggi (Saami Parliament) in Norway, the Barents Secretariat, and the Norwegian Cultural Council, supported this cooperation

---

[41] In Norway, this is highlighted in Penal Code 1902 § 162 as well as Penal Code 2005 § 231.
[42] Allemannsretten – regjeringen.no. Similarly in Finland, www.luontoon.fi/jokamiehenoikeudet.

financially and described the festival as an important arena for intercultural negotiations (see Brattland & Myrvoll 2014).

The leader of the festival, Ronald Kvernmo, was also the first person to establish his own chaga business, where chaga is presented as a product with many uses that extend from the health sector all the way into the tourism sector. In our conversation about how the idea of an independent chaga company took shape, collaboration with cultural workers from the Russian side of Sápmi,[43] which occurred at the Isogaisa festival, was highlighted as a decisive factor. Kvernmo elaborates:

> Saami people have used the product for a very long time. But you know because of the hard assimilation politics, language, culture, and religion were forced to disappear. In this process, Saami traditional knowledge – knowledge about nature, about plants, and fungi that had health-promoting effects – was also lost. Now it is my task to bring this knowledge forth. It is in many ways about a renovation of the culture – and about renovating Saami business life which is about the ability to make a living from nature. That is what I do but adapted to our time, to be able to live on what I find in nature. (Kvernmo 2020b)

Kvernmo highlights Isogaisa as a learning arena in which a dynamic process of remembering brings forth elements from the past, including the use of chaga. The venue generates an understanding that traditions that have been lost due to colonization and assimilation politics can be shared and retrieved through knowledge exchange with tradition bearers from other areas within Sápmi.

Kvernmo's chaga entrepreneurship brings alive patterns of knowledge and practice transmitted from encounters with Indigenous peoples across Sápmi, making them meaningful in a local context where chaga is understood as part of a common, but partly lost, cultural heritage, at least in Rivták. Johnson and Kraft refer to this process as "scalar translations" (2017: 6-7, italics in original: see also Kraft 2022), "ways in which locally specific objects and actions gain relevance outside of their site-specific locations and contexts, as belonging to the broader Indigenous *we* and *our*, and – vice versa – how globalizing idioms are anchored in the local *we*."

Thus, Kvernmo's chaga enterprise reveals the scalar range of this mushroom, providing new meanings to religious diffusion. An element from an extended Indigenous *we* – in this case from Sápmi on the Russian side – is being reclaimed and cultivated as a local Indigenous shamanic tradition. Sápmi is a geographical area characterized by huge distances; 1100 km separate Rivták

---

[43] Chaga has a long cultural history as medicine in Russia; there are written sources from around 1600 that mention this growth. The one in particular who made the fungus known outside Russia was Aleksandr Solzhenitsyn, who in the novel *The Cancer Ward* (1968) points out that the main character uses chaga as a medicine for cancer.

from Lovozero in Murmansk, and the fourteen-hour car ride involves crossing several national borders – Sweden, Finland, and Russia. Through Kvernmo's entrepreneurship, chaga traditions from the Russian side of Sápmi and contemporary shamanic religious practices in Norway are fused together, despite the great distances, and serve to open new cultural, economic, and political horizons. This fusion reinforces the image of shamanism as an Indigenous religion and, not least, as a nature religion.

Kvernmo's Chaga Shamanship

Kvernmo's chaga enterprise is a multidimensional and innovative concept; it belongs to a type of entrepreneurship that expands contemporary understandings of public spaces for religion. As Thomas Karl Alberts notes:

> [T]he emergence in recent decades of a specifically neoliberal homo economicus has transformed some shamans into spiritual entrepreneurs whose investments in their embodied human capital – in their skills and experience, social and spiritual networks, and related qualities of their corporeal being – render their shamanic practice as a form of economic self-conduct. (Alberts 2015: 2.)

As a shaman-entrepreneur, Kvernmo transforms shamanism into capital. The commodities that are made available for consumers, however, are not only controlled by Kvernmo but also targeted and affected by public authorities and public legislation.

Kvernmo chose to combine his shaman studies with a bachelor's degree in marketing from the Norwegian Business School, in which he explored the possibilities of developing a shaman business in a local community in northern Norway. In his thesis, which he wrote together with Kent Ove Alte, Kvernmo highlights shamanism as part of Saami cultural heritage. Furthermore, they refer to shamanism as an innate Saami competence (Alte & Kvernmo 2009: 9). Kvernmo's vision, as stated in the thesis, is to create history's most talked about shamanic center, where the main income will come from accommodations, along with courses, shamanic activities, and food services (Alte & Kvernmo 2009). Kvernmo's thesis reflects the image of the Saami as a people with a spiritual nature and, more specifically, as a people directly linked to a particular religious heritage, namely shamanism.

In 2010, Kvernmo took his studies one step further by establishing his own shaman enterprise. By adapting shamanism to a local community, as he had learned through Ailo Gaup's courses and the Isogaisa festival, as well as his studies of Saami religion at the Arctic University of Tromsø, Kvernmo developed his own multifaceted version of shamanism. The new context and different materialities supply new meanings. To be able to make a living from shamanism in this remote community, a solid and broad foundation is needed. Thus, chaga became a new central materiality and the resource on which Kvernmo's shamanic entrepreneurship is centered.

Although the business starts out small, Kvernmo quickly began to work with a local entrepreneurial company and started developing chaga into an official health food product to be distributed throughout the country. He launched his own online store, offered courses in shamanism in which chaga plays a central part, wrote a book, and now publishes weekly newsletters and organizes radio programs on shamanism from his own living room. Together with his wife, Beate Sandjord, Kvernmo eventually entered the tourism market with a product that combined chaga, shamanism, dog sledding, and the northern lights. This multidimensional chaga business reveals how a semireligious enterprise takes shape, highlighting the complex and shifting relationship between the secular and the sacred. Kvernmo's enterprise clearly illuminates the ways that shamanism expands the circles traditionally viewed as religiously and spiritually relevant and claims attention and space. What is new in this example is the area in which this semireligious entrepreneurship unfolds – a region in which Christianity and Læstadianism have dominated the local religious landscape. Also new is the revitalization of translocal Saami worldviews and traditions.

As early as 2015, the national newspaper *Verdens Gang* (VG) announced that a Saami shaman was making a living off a sacred mushroom (Christiansen 2015). The photograph as well as the media story itself fed contemporary discourses promoting Indigenous people as living in harmony with nature, as eco-friendly, natural, authentic, and creative (Mathisen 2004, 2003; Valkonen & Valkonen 2014; Chandler & Reid 2019). In the newspaper article, Kvernmo is seen holding his drum high, and in the background, there is a birch forest potentially holding chaga (Fig. 15). This positive attention stands in stark contrast to how the media in general have covered alternative spiritualities, such as New Age events and entrepreneurs (Kraft 2011: 105). Unlike New Age entrepreneurs, who often are pictured as naive and unreliable social actors, shamans are depicted as spiritually responsible, identifying with collective needs and the requirements of environmentalism, bent upon reviving Saami Indigenous religious traditions (see also Kalvig 2015).

The logic of the market and the media are factors and processes changing the religious landscape. Kvernmo's shaman enterprise reveals that shamanism has ramifications beyond a limited spiritual environment. At the same time, this creativity is also closely related to and interwoven with the place Kvernmo has chosen for his business. His remote farm, surrounded by the high Rivták mountains, relies on a different form of creativity than that needed in a larger city for the entrepreneur to be able to survive as a shaman. Kvernmo's entrepreneurship takes shape through the selection and interpretation of the "local place" and the

Figure 15 Kvernmo with his drum held high and, in the background, a birch forest potentially containing chaga. Photo by Veslemøy Einteig Christiansen, used by permission.

"traditional," and through the effect of different events, practices, and materialities that are noted as particularly meaningful. This narrative underpins and develops discourse about Indigenous religion by presenting Saami cultures as spiritual, close to nature, in balance with the natural elements, and following ancient traditions.

The Regulating and Legitimizing of Chaga

The demand for chaga gradually increased in line with Kvernmo's marketing.[44] Initially, he had no coproducers and was responsible for the entire production process himself – from harvesting to drying the mushroom, grinding it to powder, and packing, marketing, religionizing, and selling it. The most important sales arenas were religious: the Isogaisa festival, as well as the alternative fairs, which took place in cities all over Norway in which alternative therapists could sell their product and services to the public (see Kraft 2009). Kvernmo had

---

[44] In our conversations, Kvernmo was concerned with conveying that his way of harvesting chaga is sustainable and that he always leaves a piece of the fungus behind during harvest so that it has the opportunity to grow back. Some still question this perspective and argue that there are limits to how much chaga one can harvest and still maintain a sustainable stock. In Finland, the commercial value of chaga has been seen as so significant that there is even a recent book on how to grow chaga and make money (Helenius & Kyhälä 2020: *Pakuri: Kasvata ja tienaa*).

Figure 16 Chaga bottles by BIOFORM with symbols from the Saami drums, such as the reindeer, a Saami deity holding a drum, and the logo of the Isogaisa festival. Photo by Ronald Kvernmo (used by permission).

his own chaga stand at these venues, where visitors were offered a tasting and informed about chaga's healing powers as well as its relations to shamanism.

Due to the heavy workload, Kvernmo began looking for possible organizations with which to cooperate. The local health care manufacturer in the municipality Ráisavuona (Sørreisa) close to Rivták, BIOFORM, stood out as a natural partner. With the company's business and marketing competence, Kvernmo was able to develop a health care product that could be distributed widely. Central marketing symbols displayed on the label are the northern lights, symbols from the Saami drums such as the reindeer, a Saami deity holding a drum, and the logo of the Isogaisa festival (Fig. 16). In collaboration with BIOFORM, a secular–sacred product emerged that is marketed as related to Saami culture as well as to Saami spirituality:

> According to Sami folklore, chaga is a sacred drink. In Sami it is called báhkkol or báhkkololmmai. Translated, báhkkololmmai means the chagaman or chaga people. That is, the underground people who live in the forest and are connected to the power of chaga. It is not without reason that chaga is a sacred drink, and that it is considered a very powerful "spirit." Chaga was used to treat a wide range of diseases, disorders, and injuries. And it worked![45]

The label and sales pitch marketed on Kvernmo's website evokes chaga as something more than a dietary supplement: it is presented as a product with spiritual properties. The nature spirituality appearing on the label is enhanced

---

[45] https://isogaisa.org/chaga-info/.

through references to science, thereby amplifying chaga's benefits. The newsletters that Kvernmo sends out weekly are filled with stories in which scientific and spiritual truth-seeking are interwoven. One newsletter explains chaga's high level of antioxidants:

> But why do we need antioxidants? First and foremost, they protect against the **"free radicals."** Free radicals are simply molecules that have lost or gained one extra electron and that can attack our cells . . . . Antioxidants protect the cells against such free radicals. The content of antioxidants is calculated in ORAC per gram (Oxygen Radical Absorbance Capacity). Antioxidants are found in some foods. For example, blueberries contain 24 ORAC/gram and pomegranate 105 ORAC/gram, which is quite a lot. **Chaga extract contains 1104 ORAC / gram!!** This is another one of chaga's amazing properties! (Kvernmo 2020a; our translation; boldface in original.)

Referring to scientific experiments and imitating scientific language and style are well-known legitimizing strategies within contemporary religions (see Hammer 2001; Rothstein 2004). Presenting the ORAC per gram in chaga in scientific language with complex arguments makes the product appear almost magical. The marketing of chaga invokes even more than the rationality and authenticity of science by suggesting the "magnetic aura" associated with science (see Lewis 2010: 26). On the label of the chaga bottle and in the newsletter, science and magic come together to serve a joint cause, namely, to reinforce the impression of chaga as a product capable of working magic and bringing health.

Kvernmo's commercial mushroom collecting gives a glimpse at the seams of global capitalism as well as the entanglement of religion and capitalism. The economic dimension is crucial to understanding these types of entrepreneurship dynamics, where the dissemination of religion occurs quite literally in the marketplace. The marketplace is itself an organizational element that guides spiritual entrepreneurship. Whereas a church or institution forms the structural element of spiritual life in other religions, in the case of shamanic practices, commercialism itself is an organizational element that provides important regulations and guidelines.

By selecting chaga as the primary product and experience in his shaman enterprise, Kvernmo is obliged to follow a set of official regulations and guidelines. "If one is to sell chaga for consumption and as medicine," he says," there are very strict requirements regarding the production premises and the production itself. For example, I had to register my company and get approval from the Norwegian Food Safety Authority, if I wanted to serve chaga" (Kvernmo 2020b).

The Norwegian Food Safety Authority (Mattilsynet), which establishes the guidelines governing the production of chaga, and BIOFORM are the secular actors that play a central role in regulating how and under what conditions and into what format a chaga shaman entrepreneurship can evolve. They affect the limitations and opportunities of chaga as a shamanic product and as an element in contemporary Nordic shamanism. Together with the Sámediggi, the Cultural Council, and the Barents Secretariat, which allocate funds for a pan-Saami collaboration, the Norwegian Food Safety Authority and the production company BIOFORM contribute to the formation and recognition of how chaga as a shaman product may occur.

Establishing Chaga as an Element of Folk Medicine in Cooperation with the Chaga Spirit, Báhkkololmmai

Additional institutions and firms are also contributing to regulating Ronald Kvernmo's chaga shamanship. According to him, the chaga mushroom is infused with its own spiritual agency. In northern Saami, chaga is known as Báhkkololmmai. Olmai is a linguistic suffix found in several of the Saami gods' names, such as the wind god (Bieggolmmái) and the hunting god (Leaibolmmái). Inspired by several sources, including his own experiences with harvesting chaga, Kvernmo describes chaga as a spirit, or more precisely as a spiritual people, giving a detailed description of Báhkkololmmai's characteristics and abilities:

> Báhkkololmai, the chaga spirit, lives in the forest. It is a force that represents the chaga mushroom. And you know Saami spirits. Most Saami spirits have a dual role, they are good, but they also hold an aspect of trouble and chaos. The wind god, for example, can blow away the mosquitoes, but he can also take lives. In this regard, the chaga spirit behaves a bit differently. It can only give us a gift and cannot do any harm in the same way as the wind god. However, the chaga spirit can be offended and especially during harvest – for example, if you remove the entire chaga mushroom so that it does not have the ability to grow back. You must always leave a piece on the trunk so that it can reproduce itself. And you must always express gratitude for the gift you receive by performing a small ceremony. (Kvernmo 2020b)

Extrapolating from Kvernmo's knowledge, experiences, and his interactions with nature, a Saami spiritual being makes itself known. This is a being that shares some of the same characteristics as the ancient Saami gods, in addition to the linguistic resemblance. It creates an arena for faith and action and serves to confirm the ideas contained in tales about Saami spirits (see also Alver 2006). Kvernmo's mushroom harvesting opens the possibility for interaction and co-creation of the chaga product together with the spirit of the chaga mushroom, which, in terms of foraging, has become a religious force that regulates not only the harvesting of the chaga mushroom but also the human relationship with nature. By giving life to chaga as a mythological being, a re-enchantment of nature takes place (see Gilje 1998). The landscape confirms and reflects myths and stories about the chaga people. In this process, nature is charged with not only people's personal stories and memories, but also links to a Saami past and to the spiritual beings incorporated in this past – from which Báhkkololmmai derives its nourishment.

In addition to addressing and legitimizing the past, the chaga spirit responds to some of the challenges people in our time face, such as overconsumption and climate challenges. According to Kvernmo, Báhkkololmmai is a conscious spirit that yields insights into contemporary climate threats and has the power to teach people about a more sustainable relationship with nature. Báhkkololmmai represents a Saamification of the landscape and of Kvernmo's enterprise itself in terms of continuity, belonging, and spirituality. As such, there is a political dimension to the rise of Báhkkololmmai. The chaga spirit instantiates a political and performative conception of Saami culture as one with a special and harmonious relationship to nature, and the Saami as a people with ecological wisdom. Similar views have been cultivated and circulated in the media, in tourism, and in global environmental discourses, as well as in the Saami communities, and seem to accommodate tangled relations between philosophy, spirituality, and the "wisdom of life" (Magga-Hætta 2001; Mathisen 2003, 2004; Valkonen & Valkonen 2014: 27).[46] By focusing on the chaga spirit in the harvesting, Báhkkololmmai also serves to legitimize Kvernmo's business as a traditional and sustainable Saami practice, as an enterprise that does not exploit nature but rather maintains an ecological relationship with the chaga forest.

Communication with the chaga spirit is achieved through a thanksgiving ceremony, and thus Báhkkololmmai has also become a starting point for religious practices. As Kvernmo points out, Báhkkololmmai requires a ritual in which one expresses gratitude for the gift that the mushroom represents. This ceremony draws on Saami sacrificial ceremonies known through various source texts and adapts them to a contemporary context. Kvernmo usually performs this ceremony by lighting a fire and giving a thanksgiving offering to the fire in the form of some food or drink. Kvernmo points out:

> And this thanksgiving sacrifice is concerned with respecting nature and living in a way that does not harm nature, such as utilization of resources and over-harvesting. And this relates to the Sami understanding that you should not leave traces of yourself in nature. Nature must remain unchanged. (Kvernmo 2020b)

Báhkkololmmai, according to Kvernmo, represents a Saami knowledge system of how to behave, cope, and negotiate the environment. Thus, Chaga is a materiality that has opened new spiritual worlds that are adapted to

---

[46] Presentations of Saami culture as one with a special and harmonious relationship to nature have been strongly criticized for communicating a static and essentializing understanding of Saami cultures (see Lehtola 2012).

contemporary discourses on nature, climate, and relationality. Báhkkololmmai is a frontier being and a climate protector. It is also a spiritual being that extends its influence far beyond a defined spiritual environment. It is a being that can take action and be activated in shifting contexts.

Chaga and Tourism

Throughout history, humankind's association with nature has changed due to cultural, economic, and political factors. It has been praised and disowned, and it continues to be part of a dynamic process in which it is altered and recast in changing discourses and contexts.

The link between the religious experience and the nature experience has become a highly visible bond in the marketing of the "high north" as a tourist destination. The phrase "arctic magic" is frequently used in tourism marketing today and has in the last decade been established as a common ingredient in promotional materials, with the northern Norwegian region constructed as an arctic region, situated near the borders of civilization (Bæck & Paulgaard 2012; similarly in Finland, e.g., Herva et al. 2020). For Kvernmo, tourism has become an alternative livelihood and an important source of income. The construction of chaga as a main element in tourism entrepreneurship makes it fit exceptionally well into these contemporary structures of needs and motivations in different cultural areas beyond the religious-spiritual field. Kvernmo points out:

> Yes, of course we use chaga and present it to the visiting tourist. I make a big deal out of it. . . . The ceremony that we do with chaga is something tourists love. We do a chaga ceremony to strengthen ourselves before we meet the northern lights. They like it. . . . We drink chaga to strengthen ourselves to meet our ancestors.

Fonneland: What do you tell them about chaga?

Kvernmo: What do I tell them? I ask them to close their eyes and imagine that they are walking in a large, moist birch forest, with large birch trees on all sides, and with soft grass under their legs. Then I ask them to look for movements in the grass and what they see then, is the Chaga people. They are shy, they are small, and they hide from humans. But when the chaga man puts his hands on the birch trunk, a chaga mushroom starts growing. It is a gift from the Chaga people, and you must reap it with respect and thank the Chaga people. Then I ask them to smell the chaga drink that they have been given. And then they smell the forest. And when they drink, I ask them to feel how the body is filled with energy from the forest and from the Chaga people. This is what I tell the tourists. (Kvernmo 2020b)

In Kvernmo's shaman entrepreneurship, religious experiences, nature experiences, and tourism are constantly co-constituted, with chaga serving as their main binder. Through the chaga ceremony, tourists inhale the forest and nature directly through drinking chaga. Behind closed eyes, the chaga spirit appears to them and prepares them to open their eyes to ancestors who dance in the northern lights. The chaga ceremony prior to seeing the northern lights creates the tourism experience as both a defining and transformative experience. The chaga ceremony is the kind of moment where effects make things matter, where a complex chain of relations is instantly felt and made tangible, and where the tourism experience has the potential to evoke the context of shamanism. The link between tourism and religion has long been debated in anthropological, sociological, and religious historical research on tourism (MacCannell 1976; Graburn 1989; Stausberg 2011). Shamanism, chaga, and northern lights represent an aesthetic that focuses on a personal interaction with nature and a marketing strategy that breaks with everyday routines and that is both in demand and unique. The chaga experience, as well as the chaga product itself with its connected story about nature, sustainability, and indigenism, can then be lifted out of its local context as souvenirs that the tourists can bring back home and activate in their own home communities.

Conclusion

Chaga has emerged as a flexible, multivalent symbol of Nordic shamanism, pressed into service for a variety of causes. It is a materiality that has enabled new concepts, rituals, and a new economy within the shamanic environment.

Kvernmo's entrepreneurship reveals how chaga has been reclaimed, cultivated, and upscaled to become a symbol of Saami shamanism, sustainability, and Indigenous knowledge. This symbol is marketed through a diverse set of arenas and takes shape as a health care product, as a spiritual being, as a ceremony, as a tourist experience, a souvenir, and as cultural capital. Chaga complicates common concepts of what religion might be, how it might be, and what it might do. It is a complex relational object that has become constituted to do work across divergent domains and worlds. With chaga at the center, Kvernmo's enterprise has emerged as a cultural force with social and economic implications that extend far beyond the local Saami community.

5 Shamanic Materialities in Finland and Norway: Concluding Observations

In the wake of the growth of shamanism in Nordic countries, a variety of hybrid materialities have been established, catering to broader audiences and meeting a variety of needs (see also Fonneland & Kraft 2013). The drums, deposits at sacrificial sites, power animals, and the mushroom chaga examined in this Element are all shaped by the contemporary category of shamanism and its networks. The construction of the category shamanism makes shamanic materialities come to life and facilitates constantly formative scalar translations between the local and global, past and present, time and space. As David Chidester accurately points out, "[M]aterial objects do not stand alone. They are engaged in practice, entangled in relations, and embedded in discourse. In the sensory register of religious discourse, embodied metaphors are an integral part of the stuff of material religion" (Chidester 2018: 207). Our explorations of shamanic materialities throughout this Element are closely linked to circulations and dynamics of categories and discourses.

The drum, sacrificial sites, power animals, and chaga are core components within contemporary shamanism in the Nordic countries, deeply entangled in processes of religion- and history-making. Religion-making is expressed in diverse fields and emerges from various positions of power that also comprise secular institutions (Dressler & Mandair 2011; Dressler 2019). Drawing on the concepts of shaman and shamanism that came to life as a result of translation processes over time and across space (see Znamenski 2007; Rydving 2011; Johnson & Kraft 2017; Nikanorova 2022) and scholarly discourses on religion, Harner and his Foundation for Shamanic Studies became a worldwide authority and instrument of regulation or accountability when it came to the field of shamanism. As we have shown, this global construct provided influences on local grounds and became fertile soil for homegrown branches to expand upon in dialogue with surrounding political, economic, and social forces. From these branches a myriad of shamanic materialities have sprung. The drum, deposits at the sacrificial sites, power animals, and the chaga mushroom are but a few of the shamanic materialities that have come to life as a result of these processes.

The region-specific aspects of shamanism also become evident when examining the ways that local histories are employed as a resource in the shaping of shamanic materialities. In Nordic shamanism, this often refers to seeking inspiration from and roots in the Saami past, but in Finland, there is also a turn to a shamanistic Finno-Ugric past, of which the Kalevala poems are seen as evidence of shamanic roots and continuity. Kalevalaicity refers to cultural features perceived as ancient and genuinely Finnish (Haapoja-Mäkelä 2019). The connections made to a Saami and Finnish past, to Kalevala, and to shamanism can be seen as an example of local history-making with direct influence on religion-making. In the process of history-making, the past is activated as a resource in local shaman entrepreneurship and in shamanic materialities catering to spiritual experiences, entertainment, and tourism.

We have tried to elaborate throughout not only how the various materialities are acted upon but also how the drums, sacrificial sites, power animals, and mushrooms have become actors in their own right, such that they influence how shamanism takes shape in local climates. The shamanism materialities have enabled new concepts, rituals, spiritual beings, and economies that direct how shamanism is expressed and takes shape. By challenging the secular–religious divide, the shamanic materialities reveal how shamanism operates beyond established religious environments. This Element also shows how shamanic materialities may influence the tourism industry, local economies, and popular culture. As Beckford repeatedly suggested, "religion has become adrift from its former points of anchorages" (Beckford 2003: 166). This does not mean that religion is disappearing, but rather that, in contemporary society, it is being altered and transformed thanks to shifting sociocultural conditions.

Shaman entrepreneurships have become established types of shamanism and hubs for the formalization and shaping of shamanic materialities. They seem to be more available in Norway than in Finland, while in Finland shamanistic elements and materialities are more widespread in commercial use and popular culture. It is not always easy to draw a line between spiritual and other uses of shamanistic materiality, as is demonstrated by how power animal cards are aimed at people seeking personal growth and how power animals are activated in workshops for children learning graphic art.

This Element acknowledges that the drums, sacrificial sites, power animals, and mushrooms do not just circulate between the global and the local. To grasp the scope of contemporary shamanic materialities, their local climates must be considered. The shamanic materialities are not neutral but are rather entangled in and in dialogue with local, social, economic, and political trends and tensions (see also Chidester 2018: 9; Strmiska 2018: 10). This Element demonstrates how shamanic materialities adapt to and are influenced by local conventions, lines of authority, and landscapes. Spotlighting the local setting, climate, and local politics is necessary, precisely to be able to grasp the domestic traits of shamanic materialities. Investigating these types of dynamics also opens new ways of inquiring into religious change, mobility, and diffusion.

The shamanic materialities in Nordic countries reveal how dynamic interactions between spirituality, Indigenous cultures, and nature are constantly invoked in the construction of the drum, the sacrificial site, power animals, and the chaga mushroom. The powers of the materialities are expressed by shifting connections to nature, to Indigenous cultures, and to a prevalent shamanic spirituality that together reaffirm a certain quality and authenticity. As such, these types of materialities feed contemporary discourses promoting Indigenous people as living in harmony with nature, as eco-friendly, natural, authentic, and creative (Mathisen 2004, 2003; Valkonen & Valkonen 2014; Chandler & Reid 2019). In other words, an eco-spiritual politics of indigenism has emerged as sought-after cultural capital that encloses the shamanistic materialities in characteristics that have value both within and beyond contemporary shamanic environments. Through shamanic materialities, this discourse can also be approached as objects that one can bring out of their original setting and enshrine in new contexts.

Shamanism can also be seen as something multicultural, universal, and corresponding to Harner's project of making shamanism available to a wide Western audience. These perspectives are evident at the Isogaisa gathering and are also emphasized by several of our interviewees: "Shamanistic drumming is a technique, drumming helps to move in the spirit World, not connected to ethnicity or Saaminess. . . . The world is shared for everybody, but ethnicity can show in ceremonial practices and instruments."[47]

The shamanic materialities discussed in this Element have become part of the tourism industry in both Norway and Finland. Drums are found in souvenir shops, its symbols are used as decorative motifs on bedsheets and pillows in tourist hotels, and power animals appear on posters, clothes, and jewelry. Sacrificial sites are visited by tourists individually or as a part of a "Lappish baptism," and artificial sieidi stones are used as decoration. In the current political context, this generating of tourists' interests and desires through marketing of Indigenous spirituality has some wider implications (Hall 2007). Several researchers point out challenges associated with this type of identity construction, which takes shape within the framework of a global tourism industry where power relationships are played out and cultural identities contested. It is argued that the creation of an Indigenous spiritual identity in a tourism context contributes to a geopolitical discourse that opens up the aestheticization, exotification, or even museumification of Indigenous cultures (Ivakhiv 2003; Coats 2011). In these settings, Indigenous people appear as representatives of a timeless tradition, holding spiritual wisdom and providing a sacred geography that can offer travelers salvation from hectic Western everyday life. However, in this cultivation of the non-Western other, "they" are always expected to live up to the image "we" create of them – in this case as bearers of traditional knowledge and wisdom, as spiritual advisers, and as men and women living in harmony with nature and each other (Ivakhiv 2003: 99).

The tourism industry in Finland has been particularly criticized for its tendency to exploit Saami culture and for commercializing vulnerable religious symbols

---

[47] Anonymous, telephone conversation with T. Äikäs, June 1, 2022. See also Eirik Myrhaug, https://sverigesradio.se/artikel/samiska-mytologin-en-rikedom-om-vi-tolkar-den-pa-nytt.

(Flemmen & Kramvig 2016; Kramvig & Flemmen 2018; Mathisen 2020; Jaakkola 2022). New cultural policies, like the 2018 report made by the Saami Parliament in Finland, can alter this trend and indicate a turning point in public discourse concerning Saami peoples' right for cultural respect, thereby ensuring that the development of Saami tourism takes place in collaboration with Saami administrative agencies, organizations, and local tourism entrepreneurs.

We hope that we have been able to demonstrate some of the complexity and dynamics of the shamanic materialities and how they are involved in processes that we have identified as religion-making and history-making. By exploring how drums, deposits at sacrificial sites, power animals, and mushrooms contribute to the development of Nordic shamanism, we have aimed at mapping how categories and materialities mutually feed into each other and take part in outlining local and constantly evolving expressions of shamanism.

References

Aarnio, S. n.d. "Johannes Setälä – suomalainen samaani." Neljä Tuulta. https://fourwinds.fi/johannes-setala/.

Äikäs, T. 2012. "Tupakoivat, laulavat ja liikkuvat kivet: Kommunikointia seitojen kanssa." In *Saamenmaa: Kulttuuritieteellisiä näkökulmia*, eds. V.-P. Lehtola, U. Piela, & H. Snellman, 81–90. Helsinki: SKS.

Äikäs, T. 2015. *From Boulders to Fells: Sacred Places in the Sámi Ritual Landscape*. Translated by S. Silvonen. Monographs of the Archaeological Society of Finland 5. www.sarks.fi/masf/masf_5/masf_5.html.

Äikäs, T. 2019. "Religion of the past or living heritage? Dissemination of knowledge on Sámi religion in museums in Northern Finland." *Nordic Museology* 3: 152–68.

Äikäs, T. & M. Ahola. 2020. "Heritage of past and present: Cultural processes of heritage-making at ritual sites of Taatsi and Jönsas." In *Entangled Rituals and Beliefs: Religion in Finland and Sápmi from Stone Age to Contemporary Times*, eds. T. Äikäs & S. Lipkin, 158–80. Monographs of the Archaeological Society of Finland 8. www.sarks.fi/masf/masf_8/MASF8-7-%C3%84ik%C3%A4s&Ahola.pdf

Äikäs, T., U. Bergmann, & A.-K. Salmi. 2012. "An attempt to use blood residue analysis to identify sacrificial practices at sieidi sites." *Fennoscandia Archaeologica* 29: 23–34.

Äikäs, T. & T. Fonneland. 2021. "Animals in Saami shamanism: Power animals, symbols of art, and offerings." *Religions* 12(4): 256. https://doi.org/10.3390/rel12040256.

Äikäs T., T. Fonneland, S. Thomas, W. Perttola, & S. E. Kraft. 2018. "'Traces of our ancient religion': Meaning-making and shamanism at Sámi offering places and at the Isogaisa festival, northern Norway." In *Archaeological Sites as Space for Modern Spiritual Practice*, eds. J. Leskovar & R. Karl, 1–20. Newcastle upon Tyne: Cambridge Scholars.

Äikäs, T. & A.-K. Salmi. 2019. "Introduction: In search of Indigenous voices in the historical archaeology of colonial encounters." In *The Sound of Silence: Indigenous Perspectives on the Historical Archaeology of Colonialism*, eds. T. Äikäs & A.-K. Salmi, 1–14. New York: Berghahn Books.

Äikäs, T. & M. Spangen. 2016. "New users and changing traditions: (Re)defining Sami offering sites." *European Journal of Archaeology* 19(1): 95–121.

Äimä, F. 1903. "Muutamia muistotietoja Inarin lappalaisten vanhoista uhrimenoista." *Virittäjä* 8: 113–16.

Alberts, T. K. 2015. *Shamanism, Discourse, Modernity.* New York: Routledge.

Alte K. O. & R. Kvernmo. 2009. *Saivo Sjamansenter.* Drammen: Bacheloroppgave ved Handelshøyskolen BI.

Alver, B. G. 2006. "'Ikke det bare vand': Et kulturanalytisk perspektiv på vandets magiske dimension." *Tidsskrift for kulturforskning* 2: 21–42.

Andreassen, B.-O. & T. Fonneland. 2002. "Mellom healing og blå energi: Nyreligiøsitet i Tromsø." *DIN – Tidsskrift for religion og kultur* 4/2002 + 1/2003, 30–36.

Andreassen, B.-O. & Olsen, T. A. 2020. "'Sami religion' in Sámi curricula in RE in the Norwegian school system: An analysis of the importance of terms." *Religions* 11: 448. https://doi.org/10.3390/rel11090448.

Asad, T. 1993. *Genealogies of Religion: Discipline and Reasons of Power in Christianity and Islam.* Baltimore: Johns Hopkins University Press.

Asad, T. 2003. *Formations of the Secular: Christianity, Islam, Modernity.* Stanford: Stanford University Press.

Askeland, H. 2011. *Hovedmodeller for relasjonen mellom stat og trossamfunn: Finansiering av majoritetskirker i Europa.* KA-note 27.4.2011. [unpublished].

Aupers, S. & D. Houtman. 2006. "Beyond the spiritual supermarket: The social and public significance of new age spirituality." *Journal of Contemporary Religion* 21(2): 201–22.

Bæck, U. D. & G. Paulgaard. 2012. *Rural Futures? Finding One's Place Within Changing Labour Markets.* Stamsund: Orkana.

Beckford, J. A. 2003. *Social Theory and Religion.* Cambridge: Cambridge University Press.

Bell, C. 1992. *Ritual Theory, Ritual Practice.* New York: Oxford University Press.

Beyer, P. 1998. "Globalisation and the religion of nature." In *Nature Religion Today: Paganism in the Modern World*, eds. J. Pearson & G. Samuel, 11–21. Edinburgh: Edinburgh University Press.

Bjørklund, I. 2000. *Sápmi – Becoming a Nation.* Exhibition catalog. Tromsø University Museum.

Bjørklund, I. 2013. "Industrial impacts and Indigenous representation: Some fallacies in the Sami quest for autonomy." *Études / Inuit / Studies* 37(2): 146–160.

Blain, J. & R. Wallis. 2007. *Sacred Sites Contested Rites/Rights: Pagan Engagements with Archaeological Monuments.* Brighton : Sussex Academic Press.

Boekhoven, J. W. 2013. "Public individualism in public Dutch shamanism." In *Religion beyond Its Private Role in Modern Society*, eds. W. Hofstee & A. van der Kooij, 245–57. Leiden: Brill.

Bourdieu, P. 1973. "Cultural reproduction and social reproduction." In *Knowledge, Education and Social Change*, ed. R. Brown, 71–112. London: Tavistock.

Bowman, M. & Ü. Valk. 2012. "Vernacular religion, generic expressions and the dynamics of belief." In *Vernacular Religion in Everyday Life*, eds. M. Bowman & Ü. Valk, 1–21. London: Routledge.

Brattland, C. & M. Myrvoll. 2014. *Etiske problemstillinger ved støtte til Sámisk nyreligiøsitet*. Tromsø: Rapport NIKU, Barents Secretariat.

Carpenter, E. 1973. *Oh, What a Blow That Phantom Gave Me!* New York: Holt, Rinehart and Winston.

Carrette, J. & R. King. 2005. *Selling Spirituality: The Silent Takeover of Religion*. London: Routledge.

Castaneda, C. 1968. *The Teachings of Don Juan: A Yaqui Way of Knowledge*. Los Angeles: University of California Press.

Chandler, D. & J. Reid. 2019. *Becoming Indigenous: Governing Imaginaries in the Anthropocene*. London: Rowman & Littlefield.

Chidester, David. 2018. *Religion: Material Dynamics*. Oakland: University of California Press.

Christensen, C. 2005. "Urfolk på det Nyreligiøse markedet: en Analyse av Alternativt Nettverk." Master's thesis, University of Tromsø.

Christensen, C. 2013. *Religion som samisk identitetsmarkør: Fire studier av film*. Doctoral dissertation, University of Tromsø.

Christiansen, V. E. 2015. "Samesjamanen lever av hellig sopp." *VG Nyheter*. www.vg.no/nyheter/i/Kv98lo/samesjamanen-lever-av-hellig-sopp.

Clifford, J. 2013. *Returns: Becoming Indigenous in the Twenty-First Century*. Cambridge, MA: Harvard University Press.

Coats, C. 2011. "Spiritual tourism – promise and problems: The case of Sedona Arizona." In *Media, Spiritualties and Social Change*, eds. E. M. Hoover & M. Emerich, 117–26. New York: Continuum.

Crossland, Z. 2012. "Materiality and embodiment." In *The Oxford Handbook of Material Culture Studies*, eds. D. Hicks & M. C. Beaudry, 386–405. Oxford Handbooks Online. http://doi.org/10.1093/oxfordhb/9780199218714.013.0016.

Dressler, M. 2019. "Modes of religionization: A constructivist approach to secularity." Working Paper nr. 7, Working Paper Series of the Centre for Advanced Studies, Multiple Secularities – Beyond the West, Beyond Modernities. www.multiple-secularities.de/publications/working-papers.

Dressler, M. & A.-P. S. Mandair (eds.). 2011. *Secularism and Religion-Making*. New York: Oxford University Press.

Dunfjeld, S. 1998. S*amisk folkemedisin I dagens Norge: rapport fra seminar i regi av Institutt for sosiologi og samisk senter.* Seminar report. Tromsø November 26–27, 1998.

Duntley, M. 2015. "Spiritual tourism and frontier esotericism at Mount Shasta, California." *International Journal for the Study of New Religions* 5(2): 123–50. http://doi.org/10.1558/ijsnr.v5i2.26233.

Eliade, M. 1964. *Shamanism: Archaic Techniques of Ecstasy.* Princeton: Princeton University Press.

Eriksen, A. 1999. *Historie, Minne og Myte.* Oslo: Pax Forlag AS.

Finn, C. 1997. "'Leaving more than footprints': Modern votive offerings at Chaco Canyon prehistoric site." *Antiquity* 71: 169–78. https://doi.org/ 10.1017/S0003598X00084659.

Flemmen, A. & B. Kramvig. 2016. "What alters when the traditional costume travels? A study of affective investments in the Sápmi." In *Sensitive Objects: Affect and Material Culture,* eds. J. Frykman & M. Povrzanovic Frykman, 179–98. Lund: Nordic Academic Press.

Fonneland, T. 2010. *Samisk nysjamanisme: i dialog med for(tid) og stad.* Doctoral dissertation, University of Bergen.

Fonneland, T. 2012. "Spiritual entrepreneurship in a northern landscape, tourism, spirituality and economics." *Temenos: Nordic Journal of Comparative Religion* 48(2): 155–78.

Fonneland, T. 2015. "The festival Isogaisa: Neoshamanism in new arenas." In *Nordic NeoShamanisms,* eds. T. Fonneland, S. E. Kraft, & J. Lewis, 215–34. New York: Palgrave Macmillan.

Fonneland, T. 2017a. *Contemporary Shamanisms in Norway: Religion, Entrepreneurship and Politics.* Oxford: Oxford University Press.

Fonneland, T. 2017b. "The shamanic festival Isogaisa: Religious meaning-making in the present." In *The Brill Handbook of Indigenous Religion(s): Pathways – Being, Becoming, Back,* eds. G. Johnson & S. E. Kraft, 234–46. Leiden: Brill.

Fonneland, T. 2020. "Religion-making in the Disney feature film, *Frozen II*: Indigenous religion and dynamics of agency." *Religions* 11: 430. https://doi .org/10.3390/rel11090430.

Fonneland, T. & S. E Kraft. 2013. "New age, Sami shamanism and Indigenous spirituality." In *New Age Spirituality: Rethinking Religion,* eds. S. J. Sutcliffe & I. S. Gilhus, 132–45. Durham, NC: Acumen Publishing.

Fowler, C. 2010. "From identity and material culture to personhood and materiality." In *The Oxford Handbook of Material Culture Studies,* eds. D. Hicks & M. C. Beaudry, 352–85. Oxford: Oxford University Press.

Fowler, C. 2011. "Personhood and the body." In *The Oxford Handbook of the Archaeology of Ritual and Religion*, ed. T. Insoll, 133–50. Oxford: Oxford University Press.

Friedman, J. 1999. "Indigenous struggle and the discreet charm of the bourgeoisie." *Journal of World-Systems Research* (2): 391–411.

Frykman, J. 2002. "Place for something else: Analyzing a cultural imaginary." *Ethnologia Europa* 32(2): 47–68.

Gaup, A. 2005. *The Shamanic Zone*, trans. Lasse V. Gundersen. Oslo: Three Bear Company.

Gilhus, I. & S.E. Kraft 2019. "Introduction: New age in Norway." In *New Age in Norway*, eds. I. S. Gilhus, S. E. Kraft & J. R. Lewis, 1–18. Sheffield: Equinox.

Gilje, N. 1998. "Renessansens menneskebilde og naturoppfatning." In *Det europeiske menneske*, ed. S. Bagge, 131–56. Oslo: Gyldendal.

Graburn, N. 1989. "Tourism: The sacred journey." In *Hosts and Guests: The Anthropology of Tourism*, ed. V. Smith, 21–36. Philadelphia: University of Pennsylvania Press.

Gregorius, F. 2008. "Modern Asatro: Att konstruera etnisk och kulturell identitet." Doctoral dissertation, Lund University.

Grønaas, O., J. Halvorsen, & L. Torgersen. 1948. *Problemet Nord-Norge: statistiskøkonomisk undersøkelse av Nord-Norges andel i landets nasjonalinntekt i 1939*. Bodø: Studieselskapet for nord-norsk næringsliv.

Haapoja-Mäkelä, H. 2019. "Näkymiä suomalaiseen muinaisuuteen: Aineeton kulttuuriperintö, kalevalaisuus, paikka ja maisema." *Terra* 131(2): 97–112.

Hagen, R. 2002. "Harmløs dissenter eller djevelsk trollmann? Trolldomsprosessen mot samen Anders Poulsen i 1692." *Historisk tidsskrift* 81(2–3): 319–46. https://hdl.handle.net/10037/910.

Hagen, R. 2015. *Ved porten til helvete: Trolldomsprosessene i Finnmark*. Oslo: Cappelen Damm AS.

Hall, M. 2007. "Politics, power and Indigenous tourism." In *Tourism and Indigenous Peoples*, eds. R. Butler & T. Hinch, 305–18. Oxford: Elsevier.

Hall, S. 1992. "The question of cultural identity." In *Modernity and Its Futures*, eds. S. Hall, D. Held & T. McGrew, 274–316. Cambridge: Polity Press/ Open University.

Hammer, O. 2001. *Claiming Knowledge: Strategies of Epistemology from Theosophy to the New Age*. Leiden: Brill.

Handler, R. & J. Linnekin. 1984. "Tradition, genuine or spurious." *Journal of American Folklore* 97: 273–390.

Hansen, L. I. & B. Olsen. 2014. *Hunters in Transition: An Outline of Early Sámi History.* The Northern World 63. Leiden: Brill.

Harlin, E.-K. & I. Musta. 2019. "Myös Suomessa tulee kunnioittaa alkuperäiskansan pyhiä paikkoja." Opinion piece. *Helsingin Sanomat,* October 28. www.hs.fi/mielipide/art-2000006287430.html.

Harner, M. 1980. *The Way of the Shaman: A Guide to Power and Healing.* San Francisco: Harper & Row.

Harner, M. 2013. *Cave and Cosmos: Shamanic Encounters with Another Reality.* Berkeley, CA: North Atlantic Books.

Harrison, R. & J. Schofield. 2010. *After Modernity: Archaeological Approaches to the Contemporary Past.* Oxford: Oxford University Press.

Harvey, D. & Wallis R. 2010. *A to Z of Shamanism.* Plymouth: Scarecrow Press.

Harvey, G. 2005. *Animism: Respecting the Living World.* London: Hurst & Co.

Harvey, G. 2009. *Religions in Focus: New Approaches to Tradition and Contemporary Practices.* London: Equinox.

Heino, M. T., A. Salmi, T. Äikäs, K. Mannermaa, T. Kirkinen, M. Sablin, M., Ruokonen, M. Núñez, J. Okkonen, L. Dalen, & J. Aspi. 2020. "Reindeer from Sámi offering sites document the replacement of wild reindeer genetic lineages by domestic ones in Northern Finland starting from 1400–1600 AD." *Journal of Archaeological Science Reports* 35, 102691.

Helander-Renvall, E. 2008. "'Váisi,' the sacred wild: Transformation and dreaming in the Sami cultural context." In *Wo(men) and Bears: The Gifts of Nature, Culture and Gender Revisited,* ed. K. Kailo, 314–38. Toronto: Inanna Publications and Education.

Helenius, A. & E. Kyhälä. 2020. *Pakuri: Kasvata ja tienaa.* Helsinki: Metsäkustannus.

Herva, V.-P., A. Varnajot, & A. Pashkevich. 2020. "Bad Santa: Cultural heritage, mystification of the Arctic, and tourism as an extractive industry." *The Polar Journal* 10(2): 375–96. https://doi.org/10.1080/2154896X.2020.1783775.

Holloway, J. 2003. "Make-believe: spiritual practice, embodiment, and sacred space." *Environment and Planning A* 35: 1961–74.

Holmberg, U. 1915. *Lappalaisten uskonto. Suomen suvun uskonnot,* part II. Porvoo: Werner Söderström Osakeyhtiö.

Holtorf, C. & A. Piccini (eds.). 2011. *Contemporary Archaeologies: Excavating Now.* Frankfurt am Main: Peter Lang.

Horn, M. J. & L. M. Gurel 1981. *The Second Skin: An Interdisciplinary Study of Clothing.* 3rd ed. Boston: Houghton Mifflin.

Høst, A. n.d. "Personal path." www.shamanism.dk/about-annette.

Houlbrook, C. 2018. *The Magic of Coin-Trees from Religion to Recreation: The Roots of a Ritual.* Cham: Palgrave Macmillan.

Houlbrook, C. 2022. *"Ritual Litter" Redressed.* Magic. Cambridge: Cambridge University Press.

Hutton, R. 2001. *Shamans: Siberian Spirituality and the Western Imagination.* Hambledon: Indiana University Press.

Hymes, D. H. 1975. "Folklore's nature and the sun's myth." *The Journal of American Folklore* 88(350): 345–69.

Ikäheimo, J. & T. Äikäs. 2017. "Constructing a trumped-up future with the pastness of the present? Neo-relics and archaeological heritage." *World Archaeology* 49(3): 388–403.

Insoll, T. 2009. "Materializing performance and ritual: Decoding the archaeology of movement in Tallensi shrines in Northern Ghana." *Material Religion* 5(3): 258–311.

Insoll, T. (ed.). 2011. *The Oxford Handbook of the Archaeology of Ritual and Religion.* Oxford: Oxford University Press.

Itkonen, T. I. 1948a. *Suomen lappalaiset vuoteen 1945*, part I. Porvoo: Werner Söderström Osakeyhtiö.

Itkonen, T. I. 1948b. *Suomen lappalaiset vuoteen 1945*, part II. Porvoo: Werner Söderström Osakeyhtiö.

Ivakhiv, A. 2003. "Nature and self in new age pilgrimage." *Culture and Religion* 4(1): 93–118.

Jaakkola, S. 2022. "Joulupukki ja noitarumpu: saamelaisuus vääristyy edelleen Lapin matkailussa." A blog text, April 12. *AntroBlogi.* https://antroblogi.fi/2022/04/saamelaisuus-lapin-matkailussa/.

Johnson, G. & S. E. Kraft. 2017. "Introduction." In *Handbook of Indigenous Religion(s)*, eds. G. Johnson & S. E. Kraft, 1–24. Leiden: Brill.

Jonuks, T. & T. Äikäs. 2019. "Contemporary deposits at sacred places: Reflections on contemporary Paganism in Finland and Estonia." *Folklore: Electronic Journal of Folklore* 75: 7–46. http://folklore.ee/folklore/vol75/jonuks_aikas.pdf.

Josefsen, E. & E. Skogerbø. 2021. "Indigenous political communication in the Nordic countries." In *Power, Communication, and Politics in the Nordic Countries*, eds. E. Skogerbø, Ø. Ihlen, N. N. Kristensen, & L. Nord, 197–217. Gothenburg: Nordicom, University of Gothenburg.

Joy, F. 2014. "What influence do the old Sámi noaidi drums from Lapland play in the construction of new shaman drums by Sámi persons today?" *Folklore: Electronic Journal of Folklore* 56: 117–58.

Joy, F. 2018. *Sámi Shamanism, Cosmology and Art: As Systems of Embedded Knowledge.* Doctoral dissertation. Rovaniemi: Lapin yliopisto.

Joy, F. 2019. "Sámi cultural heritage and tourism in Finland." In *Resources, Social and Cultural Sustainabilities in the Arctic*, eds. M. Tennberg, H. Lempinen, & S. Pirnes, 144–62. London: Routledge.

Joyce, R. A. 2005. "Archaeology of the body." *The Annual Review of Anthropology* 34: 139–58.

Jussila, J. 2022. "Saamelaisten tarinoista ammentava suomalaispeli on saanut runsaasti huomiota maailmalla: oli vaikea valinta tehdä peli oman kulttuurin traumoista, sanoo käsikirjoittaja." *Helsingin Sanomat*, June 20. www.hs.fi/kulttuuri/art-2000008886581.html.

Kaaven, E. 2011. "Isogaisa dansen 2011." www.youtube.com/watch?v=wXxqa_BJCOs.

Kaikkonen, K. I. 2020. "Contextualising descriptions of noaidevuohta: Saami ritual specialists in texts written until 1871." Doctoral dissertation, University of Bergen.

Kalela, J. 2013. "History making: The historian as consultant." *Public History Review* 20: 24–41.

Kalvig, A. 2015. "Shared facilities: The fabric of shamanism, spiritualism, and therapy in a Nordic setting." In *Nordic NeoShamanisms*, eds. T. Fonneland, S. E. Kraft, & J. Lewis, 67–88. New York: Palgrave Macmillan.

Kalvig, A. 2020. "Nature and magic as representation of 'The Sami' – Sami shamanistic material in popular culture." *Religions* 11: 453. https://doi.org/10.3390/rel11090453.

Karhu, H. 2020. "Shamanismi voimistuu nykypäivän Suomessa." A blog text, September 17. *AntroBlogi*, https://antroblogi.fi/2020/09/shamanismi-voimistuu-nykypaivan-suomessa/.

Karlsen Bæck, U.-D. & G. Paulgaard. 2012. "Introduction: Choices, opportunities and coping in the face of unemployment." In *Rural Futures? Finding One's Place Within Changing Labour Markets*, eds. U.-D. Karlsen Bæck & G. Paulgaard Stamsund, 9–22. Stamsund: Orkana Akademisk.

Kehoe, A., B. 2000. *Shamans and Religion: An Anthropological Exploration in Critical Thinking*. Wisconsin: Waveland Press.

Kildal, J. 1727 [1910]. "Afguderiets dempelse." In *Källskrifter till laparnas mytologi*, ed. E. Reuterskiöld, 88–98. Stockholm: Ivar Hjeggströms boktryc-fri A.B.

King, E. F. 2010. *Material Religion and Popular Culture*. New York: Routledge.

Kouri, J. 2022. "Shamanismista." https://shamaaniseura.fi/artikkelit/34-shamanismista.

Kraft, S. E. 2000. "De nye hellig-dyrene: Om dyremennesker og menneskedyr I nyreligiøsiteten." *DIN: Tidsskrift for religion og kultur* (3): 42–47.

Kraft, S. E. 2009. "Kristendom, Sjamanisme og Urfolksspiritualitet i Norsk Sápmi." *Chaos* 51: 29–52.

Kraft, S. E. 2011. *Hva er nyreligiøsitet*. Oslo: Universitetsforlaget.

Kraft, S. E. 2020. "Spiritual activism: Saving Mother Earth in Sápmi." *Religions* 11(7): 342. https://doi.org/10.3390/rel11070342.

Kraft, S. E. 2022. *Indigenous Religion(s) in Sápmi: Reclaiming Sacred Grounds*. New York: Routledge.

Kramvig, B. & A. B. Flemmen. 2018. "Turbulent Indigenous objects: controversies around cultural appropriation and recognition of difference." *Journal of Material Culture* 24(1): 64–82.

Kulick, D. & M. E. Willson. 1992. "Echoing images: The construction of savagery among Papua New Guinean villagers." *Visual Anthropology* 5(2): 142–152.

Kuparikettu & Saure, H. 2021. *Noitakirja: Nykynoidat ja noitien historiaa*. Helsinki: Into.

Kuppikivi. n.d. "Kuppikivi." http://akp.nba.fi/wiki;kuppikivi.

Kvernmo, R. 2020a. Digital newsletter. https://isogaisasiida.mailmojo.no/m/337359/4ZGk47qRlv0vXaCJtP0NogaaaxwYEZ.

Kvernmo, R. 2020b. Zoom Interview with T. Fonneland. December 18.

Kvernmo. n.d. "Chaga inneholder 46 ganger mer antioksidanter enn blåbær!" Digital newsletter. https://isogaisasiida.mailmojo.no/m/253938/4ZGk47qRlv0vXaCJtP0NogaaaxwYEZ.

Lakkala, A. 2015. "Yhdenvertaisuusvaltuutettu suomii Visit Finlandin markkinointivideota: "Saamelaisten kulttuurisia oikeuksia on kunnioitettava matkailussa." Yle.fi, October 23 . https://yle.fi/sapmi/3-8403269.

Last, J. 2022. "*Skábma: Snowfall* is a huge win for Indigenous game makers." *Wired*, January 11. www.wired.com/story/skabma-snowfall-Indigenous-game-makers/.

Lehto – Shamanismi. n.d. "Shamanismi." https://lehto-ry.org/shamanismi.html.

Lehto – Suomen Luonnonuskontojen yhdistys ry. 2022. "Samanismi on universaali uskonto." June 15. www.facebook.com/Lehtory/posts/4806333166135110.

Lehtola, V.-P. 2012. *Saamelaiset suomalaiset: Kohtaamisia 1896–1953*. Helsinki: Suomalaisen Kirjallisuuden Seura.

Leiwo, H. 2022. "Jurvalainen Juha Järvinen vastasi mystiseen sähköpostiin, ja nyt viikinkielokuvassa The Northman soivat eteläpohjalaiset noitarummut." Yle.fi/uutiset. https://yle.fi/uutiset/3-12423143.

Lewis, J. 2010. "How religions appeal to the authority of science." In *Handbook of Religion and the Authority of Science*, eds. J. Lewis & O. Hammer, 23–40. Leiden: Brill.

Lilleslåtten, M. 2021. Vanskelig for samer å sette politisk dagsorden. www.hf .uio.no/imk/forskning/aktuelt/aktuelle-saker/2021/vanskelig-for-samer-a-sette-politisk-dagsorden.

Lucas, G. & V. Buchli. 2001. *Archaeologies of the Contemporary Past*. London: Routledge.

MacCannell, D. 1976. *The Tourist: A New Theory of the Leisure Class*. New York: Schocken Books.

Magga-Hætta T. M. 2001. "Pohjoinen luontosuhde ei ole myytävänä." *Kide* 5/ 2001: 21–22.

Manker, E. 1957. *Lapparnas heliga ställen: Kultplatser och offerkult i belysning av nordiska museets och landsantikvariernas fältundersökningar*. Acta Lapponica XIII. Stockholm: Almquist & Wiksell.

Masuzawa, T. 2005. *The Invention of World Religions: Or, How European Universalism Was Preserved in the Language of Pluralism*. Chicago: Chicago University Press.

Mathisen, S. R. 2000. "Kulturen materialisering: en innledning." In *Kulturens materialisering: identitetog uttrykk*, ed. S. R. Mathisen, 9–24. Kulturstudier 13. Kristiansand: Høyskoleforlaget.

Mathisen, S. R. 2003. "Tracing the narratives of the ecological Sami." In *Nature and Identity: Essays on the Culture of Nature*, eds. K. Pedersen & A. Viken, 189–206. Kulturstudier 36. Kristiansand: Norwegian Academic Press.

Mathisen, S. R. 2004. "Hegemonic representations of Sámi culture: From narratives of noble savage to discourses on ecological Sámi." In *Creating Diversities: Folklore, Religion and the Politics of Heritage*, eds. A.-L. Siikala, B. Klein, & S. R. Mathisen, 17–30. Helsinki: SKS.

Mathisen, S. R. 2010. "Indigenous spirituality in the touristic borderzone: Virtual performances of Sami Shamanism in Sapmi Park." *Temenos – Nordic Journal of Comparative Religion* 46(1): 53–72. https://doi.org/ 10.33356/temenos.6941.

Mathisen, S. R. 2020. "Souvenirs and the commodification of Sámi spirituality in tourism." *Religions* 11(9): 429. https://doi.org/10.3390/rel11090429.

Miller, D. 2005. *Materiality*. Durham, NC: Duke University Press.

Miller, D. 2010. *Stuff*. Cambridge: Polity Press.

Minde, H. 2008. "Constructing 'Laestadianism': A case for Sami survival?" *Acta Borealia: A Nordic Journal of Circumpolar Societies* 15(1): 5–25.

Mitchell, J. P. 2018. "Religion and embodiment." In *The International Encyclopedia of Anthropology*, ed. H. Callan, n.p. https://doi.org/10.1002/ 9781118924396.wbiea1791.

Morgan, D. 2009. *Religion and Material Culture: The Matter of Belief*. Abingdon: Routledge.

Morgan, D. 2012. *The Embodied Eye: Religious Visual Culture and the Social Life of Feeling*. Berkeley: University of California Press.

Myrhaug, E. 2018. "Sjamanveien: veien til moderne sjamanisme." *Ottar: Populærvitenskaplig tidsskrift fra Tromsø Museum-Universitetsmuseet* 321: 28–33.

Naum, M. & J. M. Nordin. 2013. "Introduction: Situating Scandinavian colonialism." In *Scandinavian Colonialism and the Rise of Modernity: Small Time Agents in a Global Arena*, eds. M. Naum & J. M. Nordin, 3–16. New York: Springer.

Nikanorova, L. 2022. "The role of academia in finding, claiming, and authorizing Sakha religions." In *Religions around the Arctic: Source Criticism and Comparison*, eds. H. Rydving & K. Kaikkonen, 255–75. Stockholm: Stockholm University Press.

Olsen, K. 2000. "Sápmi: fra Djursland til Kåfjord." In *Kulturens materialisering: identitet og uttrykk*, ed. S. R. Mathisen, 53–66. Kulturstudier 13. Kristiansand: Høyskoleforlaget.

Olsen, K. 2017. "What does the sieidi do? Tourism as a part of a continued tradition?" In *Tourism and Indigeneity in the Arctic*, eds. A. Viken & D. K. Müller, 225–45. Bristol: Channel View Publications.

Pääkkönen, L. W. 1902. "Matkakertomus muinais- ja kansatieteelliseltä keräysmatkalta kesällä 1901 Tornion, Muonion ja Ounas sekä Kemin jokivarsilla." *Selonteko muinais- ja kansatieteellisestä keräysmatkastani Tornion jokilaaksossa Oulun Historiallisen Seuran toimesta kesällä 1900*. L. Pääkkönen: Kytäjä.

Pain, R. 1965. "Læstadianisme og samfunnet." *Tidsskrift for samfunnsforskning* 1965(1): 60–73.

Partridge, C. 2004. *The Re-Enchantment of the West*. London: A Continuum Imprint.

Paulaharju, S. 1922. *Lapin muisteluksia*. Helsinki: Kustannusosakeyhtiö Kirja.

Paulaharju, S. 1932. *Seitoja ja seidan palvontaa*. Helsinki: Suomalaisen Kirjallisuuden Seura.

Peaceful. n.d. "Casket covers." www.peaceful.fi/en/tuotteet. June 21.

Peltonen, E. 2021. "Rumpuystäväni." *Minä Olen -lehti*.

Pike, S. M. 2004. *New Age and Neopagan Religion*. New York: Columbia University Press.

Prentice, R. 2001. "Experiential cultural tourism: Museums & the marketing of the new romanticism of evoked authenticity." *Museum Management and Curatorship* 19 (1): 5–26. https://doi.org/10.1080/09647770100201901.

Primiano, L. N. 1995. "Reflexivity and the study of belief." *Western Folklore* 54(1): 37–56.

Rainio, R., A. Lahelma, T. Äikäs, K. Lassfolk, & J. Okkonen. 2018. "Acoustic measurements and digital image processing suggest a link between sound rituals and sacred sites in Northern Finland." *Journal of Archaeological Method and Theory* 25(2): 453–74. https://doi.org/10.1007/s10816-017-9343-1.

Redden, G. 2005. "The new age: Towards a market model." *Journal of Contemporary Religion* 20(2): 231–46.

Roberts, B. 2004. "Biography, time and local history-making." *Rethinking History* 8(1): 89–102. https://doi.org/10.1080/13642520410001649741.

Robertson, R. 1995. "Glocalization: Time-space and homogeneity-heterogeneity." In *Global Modernities*, ed. M. Featherstone, 25–44. London: Sage.

Rothstein, M. 2004. "Science and religion in the new religions." In *The Oxford Handbook of New Religious Movements*, ed. J. R. Lewis, 99–118. Oxford: Oxford University Press.

Rountree, K. 2012. "Neo-Paganism, animism, and kinship with nature." *Journal of Contemporary Religion* 27: 305–20.

Ruotsala, H. 2008. "Does sense of place still exist?" *Journal of Ethnology and Folkloristics* 1(2): 43–54.

Rydving, H. 1991. "The Saami drums and the religious encounter in the 17th and 18th centuries." In *The Saami Shaman Drum*, eds. T. Ahlbäck & J. Bergman, 28–51. Scripta Instituti Dionneriani Aboensis 14. Stockholm: Almqvist & Wiksell International.

Rydving, H. 1993. *The End of Drum-Time: Religious Change among the Lule Saami, 1670s–1740s.* Acta Universitatis Upsaliensis. Historia Religionum 12. Uppsala: Almqvist & Wiksell.

Rydving, H. 1995. *Samisk religionshistoria: några källkritiska problem.* Uppsala Research Reports in the History of Religions 4. Stockholm: Almqvist & Wiksell International.

Rydving, H. 2010. *Tracing Sami Traditions: In Search of the Indigenous Religion Among the Western Sami During the 17th and 18th Centuries.* Oslo: Institute for Comparative Research in Human Culture / Novus.

Rydving, H. 2011. "Le chamanisme aujourd'hui: constructions et déconstructions d'une illusion scientifique." *Études mongoles et sibériennes, centrasiatiques et tibétaines* [En ligne], 42. https://doi.org/10.4000/emscat.1815.

Said, E. 1978. *Orientalism: Western Conceptions of the Orient.* New York: Pantheon Books.

Salmi, A.-K., T. Äikäs, & S. Lipkin. 2011. "Animating ritual at Sámi sacred sites in Northern Finland." *Journal of Social Archaeology* 11(2): 212–35.

Salmi, A.-K., T. Äikäs, M. Spangen, M. Fjellström, & I.-M. Mulk. 2018. "Traditions and transformations in Sámi animal offering practices." *Antiquity* 92(362): 472–89.

Salmi, A.-K., M. Fjellström, T. Äikäs, M. Spangen, M. Núñez, & K. Lidén. 2020. "Zooarchaeological and stable isotope evidence of Sámi reindeer offerings." *Journal of Archaeological Science: Reports* 29. https://doi.org/10.1016/j.jasrep.2019.102129.

Salmi, A.-K. & O. Seitsonen 2022. "Effects of reindeer domestication on society and religion." In *Domestication in Action: Past and Present Human–Reindeer Interaction in Northern Fennoscandia*, ed. A.-K. Salmi, 215–47. Cham: Palgrave Macmillan.

Schanche, A. 2004. "Horizontal and vertical perceptions of Saami landscapes." In *Landscape, Law and Customery Rights: Report from a Symposium in Guovdageaidnu-Kautokeino March 26–28, 2003*, eds. M. Jones & A. Scanche. *Dieđut* 3: 1–10.

Schøyen, C. 1943 [1918]. *Tre stammers møte*. Oslo: Gyldendal.

Setälä, J. 1997. *Shamaanin matka*. Helsinki: Delfiini Kirjat.

Setälä, J. 2000. *Shamaanin maailma*. Helsinki: Suomalaisen Mytologian Seura ry.

Setälä, J. 2005. *Shamaanin rumpu*. Helsinki: Suomalaisen Mytologian Seura ry.

Shamaaniseura ry. 2022a. "Toinen shamanistinen kokoontuminen ja konferenssi." https://shamaaniseura.fi/kokoontuminen-gathering/.

Shamaaniseura ry. 2022b. "Usein kysytyt kysymykset." https://shamaaniseura.fi/home/usein-kysytyt-kysymykset.

Sidky, H. 2010. "On the antiquity of shamanism and its role in human religiosity." *Method and Theory in the Study of Religion* 22: 68–92.

Siitonen, V. 2019. "Rumpu kurssi." www.nulituinen.fi/61004790.

Sjamanstisk Forbund. 2020. "Hva er kraftdyr og hjelpere?" www.sjamanforbundet.no/artikkel/hva-er-kraftdyr-og-hjelpere.

Smith, J. Z. 1988. *Imagining Religion: From Babylon to Jonestown*. Chicago: University of Chicago Press.

Smith, J. Z. 1998. "Religion, religions, religious." In *Critical Terms for Religious Studies*, ed. M.C. Taylor, 269–84. Chicago: University of Chicago Press.

Solbakkk, A. 2008. *Hva vi tror på: Noaidevuohta: en innføring I nordsamenes religion*. Karasjok: CálliidLágádus.

Spangen, M. & T. Äikäs. 2020. "Sacred nature: Diverging use and understanding of old Sámi offering sites in Alta, Northern Norway." *Religions* 11(317): 1–22. Special Issue, "Sámi religion: Religious identities, practices and dynamics." https://doi.org/10.3390/rel11070317.

Stark, L. 2002. *Peasants, Pilgrims, and Sacred Promises*. Helsinki: Finnish Literature Society. https://doi.org/10.21435/sff.11.

Stausberg, M. 2011. *Religion and Tourism: Crossroads, Destinations and Encounters*. London: Routledge.

Steam. n.d. "Skabma: Snowfall." https://store.steampowered.com/app/1665280/ Skabma__Snowfall/.

Steen, A. 1961. *Samenes folkemedisin*. Oslo: Universitetsforlaget.

Stoor, K. 2016. "Svenska Kyrkan och Jojken." In *De historiska relationerna mellan svenska kyrkan och samerna*, eds. D. Lindmark & O. Sundström, 711–35. En vetenskaplig antologi 2. Skellefteå: Artos.

Storm, D. 2014. "The mission networks and the religious situation." In *The Protracted Reformation in Northern Norway: Introductory Studies*, eds. L.-I. Hansen, R. Bergesen, & I. Hage, 185–210. Stamsund: Orkana Akademisk.

Strmiska, M. F. 2018. "Pagan politics in the 21st century: 'Peace and love' or 'blood and soil'?". *Pomegranate* 20(1): 5–44. https://doi.org/10.1558/ pome.35632.

Stuckrad, K. V. 2003. "Discursive study of religion: From states of the mind to communication and action." *Method and Theory in the Study of Religion* 15: 255–71.

Taigakoru. n.d. "Shamaanirumpu." www.taigakoru.fi/category/368/shamaan irumpu.

Taira, T. 2010. "Religion as a discursive technique: The politics of classifying Wicca." *Journal of Contemporary Religion* 25(3): 379–394. https://doi.org/ 10.1080/13537903.2010.516546.

Taves, A. & M. Kinsella 2018. *Religions* 9. Special Issue, "Ethnographies of worldviews/ways of life." www.mdpi.com/journal/religions/special_issues/- ethnographies.

Tukiainen, M. & Frey, M. 2018. *Pohjolan voimaeläimet*. Jyväskylä: Tuuma- kustannus.

Tweed, T. A. 2006. *Crossing and Dwelling: A Theory of Religion*. Cambridge, MA: Harvard University Press.

Tylor, E. B. 1871. *Primitive Culture: Researches into the Development of Mythology, Philosophy, Religion, Art, and Custom*. Vols I and II. London: John Murray. www.masseiana.org/primitive_culture1.htm and www.massei ana.org/primitive_culture2.htm.

Valkonen, J. & S. Valkonen. 2014. "Contesting the nature relations of Sámi culture." *Acta Borealia* 31(1): 25–40. https://doi.org/10.1080/08003831 .2014.905010.

ValonTalo, Palvelut. n.d. "Palvelut." https://lighthouseres.wixsite.com/valon talo/palvelut.

ValonTalo. 2015. "Pakurikäävän ihmeellinen maailma." https://valontalo.word press.com/, 24 February.

Vuori, K. & Backman, J. 2011. *Voimaeläimet oppainasi*. Helsinki: Delfiini Kirjat.

Wallis, R. J. 2003. *Shamans/Neo-Shamans: Ecstasy, Alternative Archaeologies and Contemporary Pagans*. London: Routledge.

Wessman, A. 2010. *Death, Destruction and Commemoration: Tracing Ritual Activities in Finnish Late Iron Age Cemeteries (AD 550–1150)*. Helsinki: Finnish Antiquarian Society.

Willumsen L. H. 2010. *Trolldomsprosessene i Finnmark: Et kildeskrift*. Bergen: Skald.

Willumsen, L. H. 2022. "The witchcraft trial against Anders Poulsen, Vadø 1692: Critical perspective." In *Religions Around the Arctic: Source Criticism and Comparisons*, eds. H. Rydving & K. Kaikkonen, 139–60. Stockholm: Stockholm University Press.

Zachariassen, K. 2012. "Samiske Nasjonale Strategar: Den Samepolitiske Opposisjonen i Finnmark, ca. 1900–1940." Doctoral dissertation, University of Tromsø.

Znamenski, A. A. 2007. *The Beauty of the Primitive: Shamanism and Western Imagination*. Oxford: Oxford University Press.

Cambridge Elements ☰

New Religious Movements

Founding Editor

†James R. Lewis

Wuhan University

The late James R. Lewis was Professor of Philosophy at Wuhan University, China. He edited or co-edited four book series, was the general editor for the *Alternative Spirituality and Religion Review,* and was the associate editor for the *Journal of Religion and Violence.* His publications include *The Cambridge Companion to Religion and Terrorism* (Cambridge University Press 2017) and *Falun Gong: Spiritual Warfare and Martyrdom* (Cambridge University Press 2018).

Series Editor

Rebecca Moore

San Diego State University

Rebecca Moore is Emerita Professor of Religious Studies at San Diego State University. She has written and edited numerous books and articles on Peoples Temple and the Jonestown tragedy. Publications include *Beyond Brainwashing: Perspectives on Cult Violence* (Cambridge University Press 2018) and *Peoples Temple and Jonestown in the Twenty-First Century* (Cambridge University Press 2022). She is reviews editor for *Nova Religio,* the quarterly journal on new and emergent religions published by the University of California Press.

About the Series

Elements in New Religious Movements go beyond cult stereotypes and popular prejudices to present new religions and their adherents in a scholarly and engaging manner. Case studies of individual groups, such as Transcendental Meditation and Scientology, provide in-depth consideration of some of the most well-known, and controversial, groups. Thematic examinations of women, children, science, technology, and other topics focus on specific issues unique to these groups. Historical analyses locate new religions in specific religious, social, political, and cultural contexts. These examinations demonstrate why some groups exist in tension with the wider society and why others live peaceably in the mainstream. The series highlights the differences, as well as the similarities, within this great variety of religious expressions. To discuss contributing to this series please contact Professor Moore, remoore@sdsu.edu.

Cambridge Elements ⁼

New Religious Movements

Elements in the Series

A full series listing is available at: www.cambridge.org/ENRM